"Anger and grie ￼
painful events in ￼
ful experiences r ￼ ...ot a lecture. Brad
demonstrates a unique level of compassion and concern
for those who are suffering. He delivers wisdom that
helps us respond to and care for those who suffer in
ways that are compassionate and practically informed."

Justin S. Holcomb, Episcopal minister; seminary
professor; author of *Rid of My Disgrace: Hope and
Healing for Victims of Sexual Assault*

"Brad Hambrick's pastoral and prophetic approach is
both comforting and incisive, providing helpful and
compelling insights for all who are navigating grief and
healing from painful experiences—especially hurt and
injustice within the church. Filled with compassionate
advice and practical tools, this book offers readers a
unique invitation to evaluate anger through a different
lens and understand how God comes alongside us in
our suffering. With clarity and grace, Hambrick takes
us on a journey of courage that will help us care for the
broken parts of ourselves and be agents of healing and
hope to the wounded along our path."

Ruth Malhotra, Writer; advocate; ministry leader

"For years I've wanted a resource that can help me provide better counsel for those who are hurting and struggling with anger at God. *Angry with God* is the book
I've been searching for. It's eminently biblical, pastoral,
and practical. I'll be giving this book out to everyone I
encounter who struggles emotionally with the problem
of evil and suffering."

Joe Carter, Associate pastor, McLean Bible Church,
Arlington, VA; senior writer, The Gospel Coalition

"Mindful of those suffering profoundly, Brad Hambrick gifts his readers with perfectly portioned, practical wisdom. He honors a sufferer's experiences, doubts, and pain while reminding us we have a patient and loving God who understands and tends to grief-filled anger. *Angry with God: An Honest Journey through Suffering and Betrayal* has already been an immeasurable blessing to my counselees."

Darby Strickland, CCEF Faculty; author of *Is it Abuse?*

"*Angry with God* provides a pastoral and wise approach to grief, and the insights and reflection questions throughout the book will benefit anyone who is experiencing the anger that often accompanies loss. As a trauma specialist, I am eager to utilize this resource with my counseling clients because it compassionately addresses the struggles they often face in their healing journeys."

Beth M. Broom, Executive Director, Christian Trauma Healing Network; care minister, The Village Church, Denton, TX

ANGRY ~~AT~~ WITH GOD

AN HONEST JOURNEY THROUGH SUFFERING AND BETRAYAL

Brad Hambrick

New
Growth
Press

newgrowthpress.com

New Growth Press, Greensboro, NC 27401
newgrowthpress.com

Cover Design: Studio Gearbox, studiogearbox.com
Interior Design and Typesetting: Gretchen Logterman

ISBN: 978-1-64507-210-2 (Print)
ISBN: 978-1-64507-211-9 (eBook)

Library of Congress Cataloging-in-Publication Data
Names: Hambrick, Brad, 1977- author.
Title: Angry with God : an honest journey through suffering and betrayal / Brad Hambrick.
Description: Greensboro, NC : New Growth Press, [2022] | Series: Ask the Christian counselor | Includes bibliographical references and index. | honest with God about your pain to restore and deepen your relationship with him"-- Provided by publisher.
Identifiers: LCCN 2022011434 (print) | LCCN 2022011435 (ebook) | ISBN 9781645072102 (print) | ISBN 9781645072119 (ebook)
Subjects: LCSH: Spirituality--Christianity. | Integrity--Religious aspects--Christianity. | Honesty. | Angry--Religious aspects--Christianity. | Pain--Religious aspects--Christianity. | Suffering--Religious aspects--Christianity.
Classification: LCC BV4501.3 .H3545 2022 (print) | LCC BV4501.3 (ebook) | DDC 248.4--dc23/eng/20220525
LC record available at https://lccn.loc.gov/2022011434
LC ebook record available at https://lccn.loc.gov/2022011435

Printed in the United States of America

29 28 27 26 25 24 23 22   1 2 3 4 5

CONTENTS

Starting Your Journey:
    Grief Stuck in the Anger Phase 1

Section 1: It's Safe to Talk About Your Anger

Chapter 1: Your Pain Is Not a Riddle 4

Chapter 2: Pacing and Preparing Yourself 7

Chapter 3: A Time Line and
    Topography of Your Pain 12

Chapter 4: A Parable of Hurt Versus Heresy 19

Chapter 5: Finding a Friend 26

Section 2: Articulating Your Pain

Chapter 6: A Psalm of Hot Lament 32

Chapter 7: What Was Good? 39

Chapter 8: What Happened? 46

Chapter 9: Angry with God
    Because of God's People? 52

Chapter 10: What Made the Pain Worse? 57

Section 3: Alleviating the Effects of Pain

Chapter 11: The Effects on Our Emotions 67

Chapter 12: The Effects on Our Thoughts 72

Chapter 13: The Effects on Our Relationships.......... 78

Chapter 14: The Effects on Our Choices 84

Chapter 15: The Effects on Our View of God........... 92

Section 4: Resolving Your Grief

Chapter 16: Valuing a Less
  Innocent Faith 99

Chapter 17: Living in the Tension of Partial
  Understanding 104

Chapter 18: Engaging "Next" 110

Chapter 19: But I'm Right!?! 115

Chapter 20: Trusting Hope Again 120

Section 5: Contextualizing Your Journey

in the Gospel

Chapter 21: Creation:
  Why We Expect Good Things 129

Chapter 22: Fall:
  Why Good Expectations Hurt 133

Chapter 23: Redemption:
  An Answer . . . Sort Of 138

Chapter 24: Sanctification:
  A Messy Journey in a Broken World 143

Chapter 25: Glorification:
  Finally, a Place of Rest 148

Appendix 1: Additional Resources
  from Author Brad Hambrick and Others 152

Endnotes 154

STARTING YOUR JOURNEY: GRIEF STUCK IN THE ANGER PHASE

No one gets mad at God for silly reasons, such as, "I wish I had blonde hair instead of brown." When we're angry with God, it is because we've faced something immensely painful. Despite our hesitancy to admit how we feel, being angry at God reveals something quite good about us. It reveals that God is important to us. We don't get and stay angry at inconsequential people in our lives. Often, we wish we cared less about God because we have a sense that it would abate the turmoil in our soul. But it is hard to care less about someone as significant as God.

In this opening paragraph, I've established two things: (1) you are hurting, and (2) God is important to you.

If you feel safe acknowledging these two things, this opens a number of possibilities. But don't feel rushed by the "if." As you read through this book, if you feel too much ground is being covered too quickly, pause. If you were rehabbing an ankle injury and had a sharp pain, you would take a break. Same thing here. The goal is recovery. The pace of recovery is determined by what facilitates your journey best.

To orient you to the journey ahead, here is a summary of the key themes we will cover:

1. Anger with God is usually a response to profoundly painful events in our lives.

2. A healthy response to profoundly painful events involves grief, and anger is an often-overlooked part of grieving; but it's possible to get stuck in the anger phase and not be able to get past it.

3. Angry grief is morally different from selfish anger; it calls for comfort, not repentance.

4. When we feel as if God is condemning us for angry grief, we feel doubly far from God: first, because of the pain, and second, because of the belief that God is upset with us because of our anger.

5. The invitation of this book is to be angry *with* God rather than *at* God—that is, to realize God wants to come alongside us to comfort us. We want to realize God is a trusted friend empathizing with our angry grief, rather than a friend-turned-enemy offended that we can't "just get over it."

6. Accepting this invitation will require courage on our part, the courage to be vulnerable again.

7. God is a good shepherd who is patient and willing to move at the pace of his sheep. God can be trusted in places that merit the name "the valley of the shadow of death" (Psalm 23).

My prayer is that this book will patiently walk with you through the process of being honest with God (and hopefully a Christian friend or two) about your pain, and that, thereby, you will find your relationship with God restored. I hope your prayers become more authentic and honest through this journey. I hope your friendship with God (Exodus 33:11) becomes stronger as you and God navigate this terrain together.

SECTION 1:
IT'S SAFE TO TALK
ABOUT YOUR ANGER

The goal of section 1 is for you to feel safe talking about painful things and the emotions that emanate from these experiences, including your anger. Sometimes, as Christians, we think we should never get angry. But God gets angry, so this can't be true.

When anger is part of our response to suffering, it is an emotional affirmation of how God sees things. Anger calls bad things bad. Not experiencing any anger in our grief is a form of dissonance between what we think ("this is bad") and what we feel ("it upsets me"). In section 1, we'll strive to resolve this dissonance.

Chapter 1

YOUR PAIN IS NOT A RIDDLE

When we're angry with God, there may be no question we ask more than "Why?" and nothing we like less than people's attempt to answer. The disorientation of painful experiences naturally takes the form of questions: Why did my child/sibling die? Why did my spouse leave? Why was that ministry leader so duplicitous? Why did my business partner betray me? Why _____?

It is as natural to ask why after painful experiences as it is for us to pull our hand back from a searing-hot pan. Putting our pain in the form of a question invites those around us to put the remedy (if that's what we're looking for) in the form of an answer. But answers may be both unsatisfying and offensive. Life is never as simple as the theological formulas we're given to reconcile the goodness of God, the power of God, and the presence of evil. Even if our Christian friends are right, their answers may not be helpful.

That's why I'm saying, "Your pain is not a riddle." Riddles have answers. Riddles start as puzzling questions. With a little deduction, the answer becomes clear. Once we see the answer, we can't unsee it. Once we know the answer, the riddle loses all its angst. It's solved.

For example, take this riddle that Gollum asks Bilbo in *The Hobbit*.

"This thing all things devours;
Birds, beasts, trees, flowers;
Gnaws iron, bites steel;
Grinds hard stones to meal;
Slays king, ruins town,
And beats mountain down."[1]

Initially, it seems complex. What is capable of doing all of these things? Then you hear the answer, "Time," and you can't unhear it. The riddle is solved. It is powerless to create unrest again.

When we approach pain like a riddle, we keep waiting for the answer that will disempower our pain. Usually, we expect the answer to come in one of two forms: (1) what we have done that is so bad to deserve this pain, or (2) what God is doing that is so good that justifies this pain. Most of our friends' responses are speculations in one of these two directions.

We can get locked into a discussion of "Why do bad things happen to good people?" The gotcha retort might be, "That only happened once [Jesus on the cross as the only fully innocent person to suffer], and he volunteered." That may be a great line in a sermon, but it doesn't answer the experience of suffering in a way that creates relief as an answer does for a riddle.

There is a clear reason it doesn't satisfy. Pain isn't a riddle. Pain is an *experience* to be processed and assimilated. Pain isn't a question to be answered. Pain is a *journey* to be traversed and endured. Trying to resolve pain with an answer is like trying to resolve appendicitis by explaining what caused the inflammation. The explanation may be accurate, but it's not helpful.

In this book, we will approach pain and the questions that emerge from it as an experience and a journey. We will grapple with biblical and theological truths along the way. There is no way to face intense pain and not grapple with a litany of God-questions. But I won't purport to give answers that result in an "aha moment" that makes things all better.

Admittedly, that may all seem a bit theoretical. Don't let that be a reason to give up. At this point, what you need to understand is this:

- I am not going to try to resolve your pain with an answer, as if it were a riddle.
- We are going to approach your pain as a life-shaping (but not necessarily life-defining) experience and a difficult journey.

If that sounds better than what you were afraid I would try to do, this has been an effective first step on our journey together. My goal in this chapter was to earn enough trust that you permit me to be a companion on the journey ahead.

QUESTIONS FOR REFLECTION

1. What have been the most frustrating or hurtful examples of people treating your pain like a riddle? How did that make you feel?

2. How does approaching your pain as a life-shaping experience or journey better fit and honor what you've gone through?

Chapter 2

PACING AND PREPARING YOURSELF

The idea of relief is exciting. If you've thawed to the possibility of this book being beneficial, you might be tempted to move through it too quickly to try to get relief faster. We don't want to do that. We want to be good stewards of this early hope so it does not become hope-deferred and make our heart sick (Proverbs 13:12).

In this chapter, we want to answer two primary questions:

1. *A Preparation Question*: How do you put yourself in the best position to complete the journey ahead?
2. *A Pacing Question*: What indicators do you need to monitor to ensure you are moving at a healthy pace?

PREPARING YOURSELF

If we know a journey is going to be strenuous, it makes sense to think through our preparation. We will consider fives ways to wisely prepare for the journey ahead.

1. *Honor Your Pacing Indicators*: If you're an efficiency-oriented overachiever, it is easy to assume that if you ace

the preparation strategies, you can ignore the pacing indicators. While this assumption is tempting, it is inaccurate.

2. *Exercise*: Most of the pacing indicators come down to managing one thing: stress. Grief intense enough to stagnate in the anger phase is stressful in a variety of ways. Few things are more effective at mitigating the effects of stress than cardiovascular exercise. Getting out for a walk, jog, or swim several times per week can do wonders for managing the stress of this journey (see the Additional Resources appendix on page 158 for more guidance on good mental health habits).

3. *Focus on Process More Than Destination*: Don't let that little voice in your head become the proverbial child in the back seat of the car repeatedly asking, "Are we there yet?" Perpetually comparing where you are to where you want to be is discouraging. So instead of disparaging yourself for how much road remains ahead of you, notice and savor each bit of progress you make. Such appreciation builds morale to continue your journey.

4. *Engage in Enjoyable Activities*: You may have heard the modern proverb, "All work and no play makes Jack a dull boy." There is a counseling equivalent, "All growth and no play makes God seem like a demanding tyrant." To offset this dynamic, identify healthy things you enjoy (the outdoors, art, reading, sports, etc.). As you engage in them, remind yourself that God delights in seeing you enjoy them—similar to a good parent watching a child play with a present.

5. *Expand Your Tolerance for Quiet and Stillness*: Both anger and pain cause us to resist quiet and stillness. The echo of what is difficult rings loud when our mind and body are still. But constant stimulation oversaturates and exhausts us. Begin with only five minutes of quiet each

day. Increase the amount as you're able. Sit still. Try not to ruminate; just let your mind settle, comparable to letting sediment fall to the bottom of a swirling glass of water set on the counter. "Be still, and know that I am God" (Psalm 46:10) is an invitation to stop wrestling against life. Accept that invitation in increments as you are able.

NOTICING YOUR PACING INDICATORS

If you learned to drive a stick shift, you remember watching the RPM gauge to see when the engine was being stressed too hard. When the RPMs rose, you learned to change gears to avoid overheating the engine. Similarly, five types of indicators reveal you are moving too fast on this journey. Remember, God is more concerned with your health than how quickly you arrive at the destination.

1. *Physical Pacing Indicators*: Listen to your body. Jesus recognized that when the body is depleted, it negatively impacts our soul (Matthew 26:40–43), and he was compassionate toward this limitation. Two of the best physical indicators are our sleep patterns and appetite. If you notice significant changes—an increase or decrease in sleep or appetite, or irritable bowel—take that as a sign to slow down.

2. *Cognitive Pacing Indicators*: Your brain can take in only so many things at a time, especially weighty things. When you have a hard time focusing, take a break. If you have a difficult time remembering important content from what you've read, allow yourself to reread that chapter without punishing yourself. Focus and retention are important cognitive indicators of how we're responding to the stress of processing painful experiences.

3. *Emotional Pacing Indicators*: Admittedly, we need to tread lightly here. You chose to engage this material because you're hurting and angry. So, use the level of agitation you've experienced recently as your baseline. If that sense of agitation spikes, give yourself the freedom to pause. Indicators of agitation might include how you respond to mistakes by others, how quickly being sad defaults to being mad, or how difficult it becomes to feel compassion for others who are experiencing hardships.

4. *Social Pacing Indicators*: When we feel overwhelmed, we tend to pull away from people. But isolation serves as insulation for our emotions. Think of a thermos; it keeps hot drinks hot and cold drinks cold. Isolation has the same effect on our emotions; it keeps intense emotions intense and muted emotions subdued. In chapter 5 we will consider how to identify good companions for this journey.

5. *Spiritual Pacing Indicators*: Arguing with God is a form of prayer. If you find yourself arguing with God, be encouraged—your prayer life may be better than you thought. But you can tell when you are arguing in hopes of a meaningful response and when you're arguing just to punish or spite the other person. The more your prayer life resembles the latter, the more this indicator is revealing you are pushing yourself too hard.

This raises the question, What should I do if an "indicator light" is flashing? First, don't freak out. You're paying more attention to these indicators now, so you can be more intentional in your response. That's good. Second, give yourself the freedom to take a break. God isn't rushing you. Don't rush yourself. Third, if a break doesn't result in the indicator lights turning off, consider talking with a counselor or mentor. There can be immense benefit to getting outside your own head when processing anger emerging from profound pain (see the Additional Resources appendix on page 158 for help finding a counselor).

Now that you've finished this chapter, rest. Don't rush to your next activity or create an implementation strategy. If you have identified a couple of ways to prevent yourself from disrupting your progress on this journey, be content and feel encouraged.

QUESTIONS FOR REFLECTION

1. Which of the five preparation strategies do you anticipate being the most valuable for you?

2. Which of the five pacing indicators do you anticipate being the most important for you?

Chapter 3

A TIME LINE AND TOPOGRAPHY OF YOUR PAIN

Now that you know how to prepare and pace yourself for the journey ahead, it's time to get underway. We will begin by looking back at the painful events at the center of your grief/anger and placing them in the wider context of your life.

For this chapter, you will do more writing than me. You'll want a separate piece of paper or journal—but please read the full chapter before you begin writing.

The premise of this chapter is that *anger and pain are messy, chaotic experiences, but healing and recovery require us to put our world back together again*. In that sense, what authenticity (i.e., anger and pain) and progress (i.e., restoring order and hope) require are in tension with each other. Both have their time and place. My hope is that this exercise begins to help you transition from raw, unprocessed authenticity toward progress.

In this exercise, you will do two things with the key events related to your pain.

1. *Create a Time Line*: This will put the "raw material" of your life in chronological order. Often our memory of painful events is glitchy and jumps

around. We lose a sense of sequence. Regaining this sense can be helpful to the grieving process (of which our anger is a part).

2. *Trace a Topography*: You may remember having a topographical globe in your elementary classroom. The mountains were raised and the valleys indented. You could feel the rise and fall with your finger. A time line is flat. But major events in our lives don't just have sequence; they also have impact. We need to trace the ups and downs of what occurred to do justice to our experiences.

Taking the time to map these life events will help you assimilate, not just understand, them. What does it mean to assimilate events? Consider how we feel when a loved one dies. Early in the stages of grieving, we resist accepting that our loved one is really gone. We don't want it to be true, and it hits us with fresh weight each time we realize it is. This is an unassimilated grief. But with time, we stop fighting against the reality of their death. We assimilate their passing into our life story. We still experience sadness, but we are not as disrupted by memories of them.

CREATING A TIME LINE

Don't get intimidated by this. Writing a history of your life can feel daunting. But all you're doing is taking the things you already rehearse mentally and putting them on paper sequentially. This exercise can have three benefits.

First, putting something on paper allows you to rehearse it less. You can edit what you write, but there isn't the need to perpetually replay it in your mind.

Second, getting everything down on paper enables you to see the whole of what you're grieving. Seeing the whole makes it clearer why your emotions fluctuate as much as they do. When you only measure your response to each individual event, no single piece seems to account for the whole of what you're feeling.

Third, it allows you to more effectively invite a trusted friend to come alongside you. If you don't have that person already, we'll soon discuss how to identify someone. This exercise is preparation for that step.

Remember, as we discussed in chapter 2, if you start to feel overwhelmed, take a break.

To help you create the time line, the writing prompts below are broken down into four time periods. Not every question or prompt may be relevant for your pain. Feel free to disregard the ones that don't fit your situation.

1. "Event(s)": Start with the key event(s) that created your pain or prompted your anger.
   - What was the day, month, or year when things went bad?
   - When did this phase begin? End?
   - If this phase of life were a chapter in a story, who would the main characters be?
   - Where did significant events take place?
   - How many key events or conversations were there?
   - Who were the innocent bystanders (if any) who didn't know what was going on?
   - Who were the fellow victims who were also hurt or offended by these events?
   - What life markers happened at the same time these things were occurring?
   - What were indicators or evidences of God's faithfulness during this time? (This will be the final question in each of the four time periods. Answer

it to the degree you are able. If the question stumps or disrupts you, don't try to force this part of the reflection until you are ready.)

This will likely be the most emotionally difficult part of the time line to write. Your goal is to create a factual, sequential history of what occurred. It doesn't have to be exhaustive. You can consider it finished when you're satisfied that, "If someone read what I've written, they would have a basic understanding of this part of my life."

2. "Before": Examine the time before the Events to help identify what made them so painful.
   - How did the relationship(s) with the key people involved develop?
   - How did the setting and context of these painful events become meaningful to you?
   - When and how did you invest in the things that were lost/damaged because of these events?
   - What seasons of life were represented in these investments?
   - What sweet memories were marred or changed by these events?
   - What kind of innocence, faith, or trust did you experience before that is hard now?
   - What were indicators or evidences of God's faithfulness during this time?

If Event(s) was the most difficult part to write, Before probably will be the saddest. Writing this material gives you a fuller realization of the good things that were damaged or lost and a clearer sense of why grief is relevant. The things that were damaged or lost had to be meaningful to you to evoke such strong emotions. Acknowledging these good things and allowing yourself to be sad about their absence is part of regaining the vulnerability necessary for emotional, relational, and spiritual health.

3. "After": Take a look at what happened after the intense Event(s) subsided.
   - What were the aftershocks and disappointments after the Event(s) time period?
   - When and how was silence painful?
   - When and how did innocent people who "just didn't know" make things worse?
   - What things did noninnocent people do to compound the pain of this time?
   - How did others create a competing narrative about what was happening?
   - What relationships were broken or faded away during this time?
   - What activities or events became less enjoyable or available during this time?
   - What were indicators or evidences of God's faithfulness during this time?

The After period may be the most misunderstood and least clear part of the time line. You were likely exhausted and emotionally threadbare during this time. Often our responses to events during the aftermath phase are disproportionate because we are responding to the cumulative effect of all that occurred.

4. "Now": The "here and now" bears the fingerprint of the "then and there." In this section of your time line, you are tracing this fingerprint as you consider the impact of what you experienced.
   - What questions do you dread being asked now?

- What people or activities do you avoid or encounter less?
- Who are the people you trust less than you should?
- What emotions do you experience more frequently? Less frequently?
- What roles or opportunities are you in less? More?
- What physical effects of your pain do you still experience? Emotional? Spiritual?
- How do you relate to the idea of trust, faith, or hope differently?
- What are indicators or evidences of God's faithfulness now?

This Now place on the time line is the starting point for the progress you will make. The work you are doing is to improve this part of the time line. Unfortunately, we can't unwrite the hurtful things of the past. But we can grieve, learn from, and assimilate them into our stories. We can reduce the impact of the then and there on the here and now. We can become both more wise and less calloused. That is the realistic benefit we can hope to gain from this book.

TRACING THE TOPOGRAPHY

There is not much new writing for you to do in this section. If you wrote your time line out in paragraph form, this is where you pick up a different color pen and begin to write numbers in the margins. You might write "+10" next to the best things in your Before section. You might write "-10" next to the most painful event. Other events will get numbers in between.

As you do this, you will see a rise and fall of hope and discouragement in the topography of your story like you experience in a well-written movie. You might, at this point, take out a separate piece of paper to create a traditional time line and make a wavy line above and below it to represent these numbers. Doing this will help you visually assimilate your memories—which have likely felt disjointed for a long time—into a cohesive story. Your life begins to come together as one story as you trace the emotional topography across a factual time line.

This exercise is complete when you can say, "This is my life. These are the things that I need to grieve and process to engage the present with hope and vitality again. This is what a trusted friend needs to know to understand how things 'move' me the way they do. If I am going to see God as good and for me, then this is the story in which I will have to do that." You don't have to be in that place now. The goal in this exercise is merely to harvest the raw material and arrange it in a way that helps you get to that place.

QUESTIONS FOR REFLECTION

1. What emotional challenges and benefits did you experience from sequencing the time line?

2. What emotional challenges and benefits did you experience from tracing the topography?

Chapter 4

A PARABLE OF HURT VERSUS HERESY

Let's start with a story. I will use this story like a parable or a metaphor. The goal is to understand how we should view the intense, unpleasant thoughts and emotions that often emerge about God during times of profound pain. We'll also consider our response to these thoughts and emotions.

The main character of our story-parable is a child. This is not meant to imply that our response to painful events is juvenile. I chose a child because we are sympathetic toward children, and I want the character you identify with in this story to be one we sympathize with. As any parable, this one oversimplifies some things to highlight its main point.

THE STORY

Imagine a child, Kendall, gets a new puppy. Kendall and the puppy bond and make many good memories, learning the game of fetch and exploring the world together, over the next several years. (This parallels the Before time period from chapter 3.)

Then someone forgets to shut the gate on the backyard fence, and the beloved dog gets out and is hit by a car. The family rushes the dog to the vet, but it's too late.

Kendall rides in the car on the way to the vet, cries in the waiting room, and is devastated when the vet finally comes out with the news. (This parallels Event[s].)

Over the next several weeks, Kendall doesn't want to play. Several friends respond to Kendall's flat affect and disinterest with, "What's wrong with you? It's just a dog. Your parents will get you another one." Kendall's grades slip because he just doesn't care anymore; grief feels overwhelming, and day-to-day responsibilities don't seem that important. (This parallels After.)

Finally, Kendall's parents see the report card and try to talk. Kendall explodes, "Get off my back! You got me the dog. You knew he would die. That means you don't care. You wanted me to feel like this. You had to know we wouldn't shut the gate every time. All you care about are my grades. You're the worst parents! I hate you! I wish I could just be by myself forever. I don't want to be part of this family!" (How to think about responses that, like Kendall's, come from our pain is the subject of this chapter.)

I hope that in this story you can see the broad brushstrokes of why we get angry with God. It may not parallel your story exactly, but I think we can ask three questions that will help us figure out what to do with the sharp and sometimes untrue things we think and feel about God in our pain.

What do we make of the emotions in this story?

Is Kendall being bad? Should Kendall be punished? Should all of Kendall's emotions be validated? Or just some of them? If so, which ones? Is anger the main thing going on in Kendall's life? It's definitely at the forefront; anger is the loudest, most obvious thing going on. But is what's at the forefront the same thing as what's "central," or primary, in a moment such as this?

What about the statements "I hate you" and "I wish I could just be by myself forever" and "I don't want to be part of this family"? How much should Kendall be asked to own these words? Should the response be different if Kendall were seventeen and had a major dating breakup or twenty-seven after Kendall's spouse died? What if Kendall is still saying these things three months later? How long, if at all, should the parents overlook slipping grades? Would the approach change if Kendall took the more active step of running away from home? We won't answer all these questions, but feeling the weight of them helps us explore our primary question of how to view our strong emotional responses to deeply painful events.

I think we can agree that Kendall is grieving, and the angry words are grief spilling over from a situation that is overwhelming. Kendall's emotions reveal important things, but if we only noticed anger, we would get the wrong impression. We would see a child headed toward delinquency and needing correction rather than a child lost in pain and needing comfort.

After profound pain, when we feel things about God such as Kendall felt about his parents, our friends often say we've crossed the line from expressing pain to being irreverent. The question we will grapple with later in this chapter is, What does God make of our emotional expressions during our profoundly painful experiences?

What do we make of the factual claims in this story?

Kendall doesn't just feel emotions. Kendall also makes factual claims. Kendall says some true things and makes some inferences.

- You got me the puppy.
- You knew the puppy would [eventually] die.

- Inference: You don't care. You wanted me to feel like this.
- You had to know the gate would [at least once] get left open.
- Inference: You only care about my grades.

We do something similar with God. We look at the facts of our situation and make inferences based on those facts. Like Kendall, when we say similar things about God, we're building our case that we have every right to be angry. This is when our friends often say we've crossed the line from expressing hurt to espousing heresy. Ultimately, the question behind the story we've been exploring is, When do we cross this line from hurt to heresy?

Some statements Kendall makes, if said about God, aren't heresy. It's true that God did know what would happen. What makes it awkward to hear is not that it's false, but that it is starting to build a case. Other things Kendall says are clearly false. The parents do care; uncaring parents usually don't buy puppies. And then, some things are just partially true. The parents do care about his grades, but that's not all they care about.

For these types of statements, the most important thing is not whether they are said or felt but whether they linger, whether we embrace them as core beliefs. A good parent can weather a storm of overwhelmed, hot grief. No rebuttal is needed. Tenderness in the moment is the best rebuttal. But if these ideas solidify from emotional reactions to firm beliefs, that is a problem.

A primary factor in whether that occurs is the parents' response. That is where we'll turn in our final question. Whether our anger is *with* or *at* God is largely determined by how we believe God responds to us in moments such as these.

How would God, as a good parent, respond?

I think it's fair to say that God wouldn't go point–counterpoint with Kendall, refuting each false claim and picking apart each inaccurate inference. Further, I don't think God would challenge the validity of Kendall's sharp emotions as being inappropriate for their parent-child relationship.

Upon what do I base this conclusion? For one thing, the sheer number of "hot laments" in the Bible. We'll develop this more in section 2, but God included many angry expressions of hurt and confusion in the Bible, which he did not feel compelled to correct. One that we'll look at in detail, if you want to preview it, is Psalm 44 (see chapter 6).

But let's return to our question. Detailing what God would not do is not the same as clarifying what God would do. The God who knows our hearts, even the parts we can't yet put into words (Romans 8:26–27), knows the difference between overwhelmed, angry grief and defiant, selfish anger. God doesn't grade us based on a list of unspeakable words or the decibel level of our prayers. God can see the heart of the person who is speaking strong words at an elevated volume.

Let's use our imagination to continue the story. Kendall, who wants to know that someone is hurting as much from his loss as he is, says, "I do. I really do hate you. You knew. You did this. I'll never forget it. I'll never get over it." What is the best negation the parents have for these claims? Soft, tender eyes that mirror his pain rather than stern eyes that seek to shut Kendall down.

This point is beautifully illustrated in *The Magician's Nephew* from the Chronicles of Narnia series by C. S. Lewis. In this book, Digory finds his way into the world of Narnia seeking a cure for his mother's cancer. There he comes face-to-face with Aslan, the majestic lion who is a figure of Jesus. Digory pleads with Aslan for a cure.

"But please, please—won't you—can't you give me something that will cure Mother?"

Up till then he [Digory] had been looking at the Lion's great feet and the huge claws on them; now, in his despair, he looked up at its face. What he saw surprised him as much as anything in his whole life. For the tawny face was bent down near his own and (wonder of wonders) great shining tears stood in the Lion's eyes. They were such big, bright tears compared with Digory's own that for a moment he felt as if the Lion must really be sorrier about his mother than he was himself.

"My son, my son," said Aslan. "I know. Grief is great. Only you and I in this land know that yet. Let us be good to one another."[2]

Digory expected Aslan's emotions to be in contradiction to his own; the majesty of Aslan's paws and claws reinforced Digory's belief that Aslan would try to overpower his pain, would put him in his place. He was surprised to find Aslan sharing his grief. Digory expected resistance (hence the "please, please"), but experienced empathy. This empathy did not cure his mother, but it did provide the foundation of trust in Aslan that Digory needed to continue his journey not knowing how it would turn out.

If we can get to that point with our pain, we will have made great progress. It is okay, like Digory, to be taken aback by God's response. When we are surprised by God's compassion, it is a reflex of praise to God, not an insult. As you consider how God responds to your pain, begin to let the main impression in your mind be the sympathy of one who knows the aches of your heart well:

For we do not have a high priest [Jesus] who is unable to sympathize with our weaknesses, but one who in every respect has been tempted [faced hard trials] as we are, yet without sin. Let us then with confidence draw near to the throne of grace, that we may receive mercy and find grace to help in time of need. (Hebrews 4:15–16)

If you can receive this image, the thoughts and feelings arising out of your pain are hurt, not heresy. In our parable, Kendall, as he sits on his bed, crying angry words in the arms of his parent, is actually refuting his own claims. He is expressing trust in the vulnerable-but-angry disclosure.

This entire book is an invitation and a process for sharing your pain *with* God as a means of processing what you currently experience as anger *at* God. My prayer is that, just as Kendall's relationship with his parents would be strengthened by a tender response from them, so your relationship with God will be strengthened as you come to know more deeply God's tenderness toward you, his hurting child.

QUESTIONS FOR REFLECTION

1. In light of your pain, what was your instinctual response to the boy in the story?

2. Hebrews 4 tells us that, because of what he endured, Jesus sympathizes with our weaknesses. How does it impact you to realize that Jesus feels sympathy when we suffer?

Chapter 5

FINDING A FRIEND

One of the most overlooked parts of the experience of anger is how lonely anger is. The heat on the outside of anger distracts from the cold isolation on the inside. This loneliness can be accounted for by at least two factors.

First, it is hard for someone else to truly know our pain. Proverbs 14:10a says, "[Only] the heart knows its own bitterness." There is a limit to how well we can describe our pain and anger. There is a limit to how well someone can resonate with what we're feeling. When we're hurt and angry, we feel alone because we know that even those who care enough to ask only "get it" to a degree.

Second, anger pushes people away. Anger makes us difficult to be around. Often, we are sharp or withdrawn when we're angry. We resist those trying to care for us. Even if we possess the self-control to avoid being rude, there is an aloofness to anger that keeps people away. Many people are simply intimidated to be around an angry or deeply hurting person.

If our faith in God has been important to us, then a third dynamic emerges: we don't want how we feel to be "contagious" and adversely affect the faith of others. If someone else is on good terms with God, we don't want to mess that up for them. We miss the innocence of what they're experiencing and don't want to disrupt it.

But that's just the from-us-to-them side of the equation. There are at least two from-them-to-us dynamics that add to the loneliness of anger.

First, some nice people aren't sturdy enough to bear the pain and hear the anger of others. They want solutions to be prompt and tidy. They want to say the right thing that makes the unrest all better. They wilt under the penetrating gaze of hard questions and internal angst.

Second, some sympathetic people are all empathy. They are a wonderful mirror to our emotions, but that's all they have to offer. They can weep with those who weep (Romans 12:15) and snarl with those who snarl, but when that is done, the conversation doesn't go anywhere else. For a moment we feel less alone, but then our distraughtness is only reinforced. This is short-term helpful but not much more than that.

Why do I bring up these challenges? Simply because they're real and we need to account for them.

FIVE QUALITIES OF A GOOD FRIEND IN DIFFICULT TIMES

With these things in mind, here are five qualities you are looking for in a friend to walk with you as you work through the rest of this book.

1. *A friend listens well even when they do not know what to say*. This is the middle ground between avoiding difficult things and being all empathy. You want someone with the humility and courage to say, "I'm not sure I fully understand yet, but I want to," or "This is really hard. I can understand why you feel stuck."

2. A friend has your best interest at heart. When we've been hurt in a way that makes us upset with God, we often have grievances about the church as well. This is a point where many Christians feel torn between caring for the individual and defending the group. We want someone who realizes that listening to us (as an individual) doesn't mean dismissing them (the church, if the church is a source of our pain).

3. A friend realizes they cannot rescue you from your hurt and anger. Caring Christians can often creep toward "doing life for" instead of "doing life with" a person who is hurting. You want someone who will honor your autonomy and not begin to try to make choices for you or tell you what you ought to think and feel.

4. A friend does not take your anger personally. You are talking to them because you trust them. You are expressing your anger and hurt to them, not at them. You are looking for someone who knows the difference.

5. A friend directs you to healthy, God-honoring choices even when you're upset. We often don't make our best decisions when we're angry. If you're about to do something that will further disrupt your life, you want someone with the backbone to say, "You can do that, but I think you'll regret it. You asked me to join you on this journey for moments like this."

HOW TO FIND A GOOD FRIEND

I hope your response to this list is, "I really want to have a friend like that. It would make a big difference." If so, here is a process for finding that kind of friend if a name doesn't immediately come to mind.

1. *Pick from the available options*. There are no per-fect friends. Even if someone does come to mind, that person won't perfectly fulfill everything listed above. An imperfect friend is better than contin-ued isolation.

2. *Ask them to be this kind of friend*. This is not the time to wait for the friendship to develop organi-cally into what you want it to be. You will need to be intentional and direct.

3. *Invite them to read this chapter*. Simply say, "I'm struggling with my faith and how I think about God. I'm reading a book to help me with that. It says a friend would be a big help. Would you read what it says about the role of a friend?"

4. *Catch them up to where you are*. If they say yes, show them your time line and topography. This both helps them get to know you better and helps you further assimilate the narrative work you did in chapter 3.

5. *Continue the rest of the journey together*. The goal is that you begin to feel less alone with your pain. As you wrestle with your unrest toward God, this friendship is a way to experience what God wants for you from the church: "Bear one anoth-er's burdens, and so fulfill the law of Christ" (Galatians 6:2).

In section 1, you have done a great deal of work. Thank you. It shows perseverance and resiliency. To this point, we have focused mainly on making preparation for the journey ahead. In section 2, we will pivot toward more overt processing of the experiences that prompted your pain. That is hard work. As you engage section 2, you will be grateful for the preparatory work you have done in section 1.

QUESTIONS FOR REFLECTION

1. Which of the challenges of finding a good friend for difficult times have you already experienced? What type of discouragement did it create for you?

2. How does understanding what it looks like to be a good friend in hard times help create hope that you could identify one or more people who would be willing to fill this role?

SECTION 2: ARTICULATING YOUR PAIN

Section 2 invites you to discuss aspects of your pain that have, for too long, not had an outlet. With any difficult topic, an invited conversation goes better than when we feel like we must force the subject. In Christian circles, when we have unpleasant emotions toward God, we feel as if what we have to say is unwelcome. We feel like we must demand to be heard. This factor, as much as any other, can cause grief to stagnate in anger.

Section 2 is an invitation, using the example of Psalm 44, to talk about the things that have left you feeling disrupted. As you read, if you start to feel emotionally overwhelmed, remember two things. First, you are free to take a break. Second, this conversation with God is an invited conversation. You are not beating on a closed door. Psalm 44 reveals you have God's full, compassionate attention for conversations such as these.

Chapter 6

A PSALM OF HOT LAMENT

We often read the Bible asking the question, *What should I think?* We come to the Bible wanting information, wanting to increase our accurate beliefs and decrease our inaccurate beliefs. There is nothing wrong with this approach. It serves us well when our focus is on cultivating sound doctrine.

But as I mentioned, cognitive understanding—solving a riddle—is not the focus of this book. We are seeking to process pain. We are seeking to assuage raw emotions. The Bible helps with that too. One of the richest places in the Bible for emotional processing is Psalms. The psalms are poetry. They are written to appeal to, give words to, and shape our emotions.

We will explore Psalm 44 section by section. It is a roller-coaster psalm. It starts up, dives low, twists through confusion, and abruptly ends with a jolt of anger. Psalms are written to provide models of communication with God, and Psalm 44 is uniquely suited to the subject of this book.

GOOD TIMES (VV. 1–8)

These first eight verses give no reason to anticipate the turmoil ahead. The psalmist is enjoying life and giving God credit for every good thing. These verses model how to respond to blessings with gratitude. But the psalmist's faithfulness in giving God credit for the good in his life confuses us later. If the psalmist was faithful here, why did things go so bad?

> O God, we have heard with our ears,
>   our fathers have told us,
> what deeds you performed in their days,
>   in the days of old:
> you with your own hand drove out the nations,
>   but them you planted;
> you afflicted the peoples,
>   but them you set free;
> for not by their own sword did they win the land,
>   nor did their own arm save them,
> but your right hand and your arm,
>   and the light of your face,
>   for you delighted in them.
> You are my King, O God;
>   ordain salvation for Jacob!
> Through you we push down our foes;
>   through your name we tread down those who
>   rise up against us.
> For not in my bow do I trust,
>   nor can my sword save me.
> But you have saved us from our foes
>   and have put to shame those who hate us.
> In God we have boasted continually,
>   and we will give thanks to your name forever.
>   *Selah*

These first eight verses teach us something about pain, grief, and anger: good times often make hard times more painful. Knowing what it is to have wealth makes poverty more disheartening. Knowing what it is to have good companionship makes loneliness more isolating. Having felt God's presence makes the sense of God's absence feel more disorienting.

BAD TIMES (VV. 9–16)

The word *selah* is used in Hebrew poetry to indicate a transition. It is not clear what occurred during the "selah" after verse 8. But whatever it was, it flipped the script on the psalmist's life. Verses 9–16 are the perfect inversion of verses 1–8. In the first section, God gets all the credit for every good thing. In this second section, God gets all the blame for every bad thing.

> But you have rejected us and disgraced us
>   and have not gone out with our armies.
> You have made us turn back from the foe,
>   and those who hate us have gotten spoil.
> You have made us like sheep for slaughter
>   and have scattered us among the nations.
> You have sold your people for a trifle,
>   demanding no high price for them.
> You have made us the taunt of our neighbors,
>   the derision and scorn of those around us.
> You have made us a byword among the nations,
>   a laughingstock among the peoples.
> All day long my disgrace is before me,
>   and shame has covered my face
> at the sound of the taunter and reviler,
>   at the sight of the enemy and the avenger.

The words that best capture your experience may be different, but they don't need to be any less honest. The psalmist is only going to get more honest as we continue. Remember, the psalms are a model for communication in various circumstances, a template for talking to God when our experience matches that of the psalmist. God wants to hear from you, and you don't have to filter your pain. We may not always be right in what we say, but God meets us where we are and begins his work from there.

CONFUSION (VV. 17–22)

In this third section, you can tell the psalmist is now grappling with the question why. He is thinking through what could have caused this tragedy. *Did I turn my back on God? No. Did I forget about God? No. Am I just deceiving myself into thinking I am better than I am? No.* This calamity doesn't make any sense. He can't find anything he's done wrong that would account for these hardships.

> All this has come upon us,
>> though we have not forgotten you,
>> and we have not been false to your covenant.
> Our heart has not turned back,
>> nor have our steps departed from your way;
> yet you have broken us in the place of jackals
>> and covered us with the shadow of death.
> If we had forgotten the name of our God
>> or spread out our hands to a foreign god,
> would not God discover this?
>> For he knows the secrets of the heart.
> Yet for your sake we are killed all the day long;
>> we are regarded as sheep to be slaughtered.

Many psalms are written with this kind of mid-journey perspective. When Psalm 44 ends, we won't know

how the calamity resolved. These psalms of incomplete
stories give words for our mid-journey experiences when
we don't know how our hardship will turn out. God is
not offended by these kinds of prayers. God knew many
of us would need a permission slip when our boiling emotions seem to border on blasphemy. Psalm 44 is your permission slip.

ANGRY, HERETICAL MIC DROP (VV. 23–26)

This section appears to cross the line into blasphemy. If it
wasn't in the Bible, we would call it heresy. The psalmist
is yelling (hence the exclamation points) false things about
God to God—accusing God of being asleep, of rejecting
his people, of forgetting. All of these are inaccurate statements about God. But they are the only explanation the
psalmist can come up with. After a demand for things to
change, the psalm ends awkwardly and abruptly. There
is no closure.

> Awake! Why are you sleeping, O Lord?
>   Rouse yourself! Do not reject us forever!
> Why do you hide your face?
>   Why do you forget our affliction and oppression?
> For our soul is bowed down to the dust;
>   our belly clings to the ground.
> Rise up; come to our help!
>   Redeem us for the sake of your steadfast love!

The natural questions are, Why is it okay for the
psalmist to talk this way? Why did God put heresy in
the Bible? What is going on here that is constructive and
redemptive for the reader? That last question unlocks the
other two. Remember, the psalms are an invitation and

template for conversation with God. Because of them the reader knows, "I can come to God with these kinds of thoughts and emotions too. God is durable enough to hear me when my heart feels like this."

God knew that sometimes heresy (false statements about God) makes better sense of life, seemingly, than truth. Psalm 44 tells us that we don't have to hide from that tension.

Think of this psalm like a parent talking to a preteen: "There are going to be times when everything I taught you seems pointless and dumb. I know it will be difficult to stick to what is wise and godly." This parental acknowl-edgment helps prepare the preteen for the emotional dis-orientation that comes when peer pressure is fierce and parental counsel seems out-of-date. Psalm 44 prepares us for the emotional disorientation that comes when we feel as if we're getting ground up in the brokenness of the world, and the Bible feels too "neat" to be useful for what we're experiencing (see the Additional Resources appen-dix on page 158 for more on praying through the Psalms).

The point of this chapter is simply, *God invites you to be honest about your pain*—the good times that made it harder, the bad times, the confusion, and even the inac-curate thoughts about God that feel convincing. God doesn't want you to be alone with your pain. God is lis-tening when answers would be premature.

The hope of Psalm 44 isn't in its content. The psalm ends with nothing but an unanswered desperate plea. *The hope of this psalm is in the relationship the dialogue reveals.* The fact that the psalmist is so mad at God reveals that the psalmist hasn't given up on God. The inclusion of the psalm in the Bible reveals that God is still present in the darkest times. In moments like these, our hope is in the one we continue to dialogue with, even when the thoughts and emotions that boil in our mind are theologically inaccurate.

QUESTIONS FOR REFLECTION

1. If you personalized your own version of Psalm 44, what would it say? What would these four sections sound like if they told your story?

2. How does it make you feel to view Psalm 44 as a template for talking to God about profoundly painful and disorienting experiences?

Chapter 7

WHAT WAS GOOD?

A couple of times, we have skimmed the surface of the question what was good? Now we will take a deeper dive. Our premise is that anger with God is often stunted grief over the loss or destruction of something good. Our anger is a declaration of how good that now-gone person, role, or thing was.

We often get stuck in our anger because we are right: it *was* good. We're not sure what to do when we're angry and we're right. Getting over it feels like admitting we are wrong when we know we're not. This is where understanding anger as part of grief gives us a sense of direction. We can be right about the goodness of what we lost without remaining stuck.

In this chapter, you will be asked to be more vulnerable than in previous chapters. Before, I asked you to be *factual*; that is, to consider the basic who, what, when, where of the good things you lost. This time, I'll ask you to be more *personal*; that is, to articulate the meaningfulness of what you lost.

INTERVIEW YOUR PAIN

Early in grief our pain crashes over us in waves. Initially, during these waves of grief, it is impossible for us to process our experience. It would be ineffective to think we are going to process an experience before we have lived it out. For example, you can't process the experience of an unwanted divorce until you live through the transitions in the months ahead.

But if you have lived through the hardship, found this book, and completed section 1, you have come to a place where just allowing the waves of angry grief to crash over your heart is eroding away at your soul.

So, how is *interviewing* different from *just listening*? If done well, both require close attention and emotional engagement; both are informative. But when we just listen, the person (or in this case, emotion) being listened to sets the agenda. When we interview someone, we are setting the agenda by asking intentional questions to get specific types of information. That is what we want to do now.

But before you begin interviewing your pain, it may be helpful to understand the concept of having a conversation with your emotions. Admittedly, it can feel weird. At its simplest level you are personifying your painful emotions.

Personifying is a way to gain some objective distance from the painful emotions. It is what the psalmist did in Psalm 43:5 as he explored his pain: "Why are you cast down, O my soul, and why are you in turmoil within me?" Too often in Christian circles we talk about the importance of preaching the gospel to ourselves (which is important) without teaching the skill of listening to the disruption we're trying to apply the gospel to.

The basic question we'll be asking is, If my pain could talk, what would it say? Or more specifically for this chapter, What parts of this experience is my pain focusing on because they were or should have been good? All the questions below explore this central question from different angles. The goal of these questions is to enable us to "hear" our pain. In relationships with others, it is rude to try to make suggestions before understanding their perspective. In relationship with our own pain, it is equally ineffective to try to change an emotion we haven't taken the time to understand.

To prepare for your interview, review two things. First, go back to your time line and topography. Review the Before time period. That is the time we want to consider. Next, review the first eight verses of Psalm 44. The psalmist's outlook in those verses is likely similar to your disposition during this Before time. The innocence of enjoying good things is often what makes us feel sucker punched by the events that created our loss.

With that in mind, here are some questions you can use to interview your pain. Of course, just as everyone's painful experiences are different, everyone's interview will look different. So, if the question that best fits your situation isn't on the list, use the list as a brainstorming exercise to find the kind of question that does fit. Remember to take breaks as needed.

- Consider the people you lost to death or relational strain.
  - Who do you miss?
  - What blessings or joys did they bring to your life?
  - What was uniquely good about your relationship with each person or group of people?

- Consider the social roles that were disrupted.
  - What did you enjoy about each role?
  - What good emerged from you fulfilling each role?

○ What relationships were facilitated by or attached to each role?

- Consider what personality traits or self-perceptions changed.
  ○ How would you have described yourself, in positive ways, before these events?
  ○ What did you like about these qualities? What advantages came with these qualities?
  ○ How did these qualities fit in with your life goals and aspirations?

- Consider the possessions you lost or how their significance was altered.
  ○ What made these things more valuable than their monetary worth?
  ○ What significance did these things have in your life?
  ○ When and how was that significance forged?

- Consider the season of life when these things occurred.
  ○ What are the normal and reasonably good expectations for this season of life?
  ○ What personal dreams or aspirations did you have for this season of life?
  ○ What current events feel different because of the disruption in that season of life?

- Consider the places where these things occurred.
  ○ What are the normal and reasonably good expectations for these places?
  ○ What other good things happen in these places that feel different now?

○ What relationships occurred in these places that you now feel less able to engage?

Your goal as you reflect on these things is to allow yourself to be more sad than mad—to grieve. As we consider these things, we want our internal experience to feel more like a funeral than a protest.

Allowing ourselves to be sad over what we have lost is an important step toward processing painful experiences. Unlike anger, which tends to keep people at arm's length, sadness invites others to come near, which allows us to feel less isolated. If being more sad than mad is still hard for you, that's okay; it is a theme we will come back to several more times. Don't rush yourself. That only pushes your grief more toward anger.

BENEFITS OF INTERVIEWING OUR PAIN

The goal of the personification exercise is to begin to change how we revere the things that were disrupted or lost. During the grief-as-anger phase, the *force of our emotions* conveyed *how important* these things were to us. Now we want to get to a place where the *clarity of our words* communicates *why* these things were important. Achieving this clarity has at least two benefits.

First, articulating the significance of the good things that were lost or damaged allows friends to empathize and care for us in new ways. It is easy for friends to get distracted by the Events of our story. When this happens, we can tell they're listening, but we still don't feel they get us. The result is that isolation persists even when we are with people who care.

That isolation exacerbates the sense of distance we feel from God.

But when we can express what has been lost or damaged, a way opens for others to empathize with our loss. Empathy from Christian friends can help dissolve the sense that God is indifferent to our pain—and thus our anger toward him can start to dissipate.

Second, being able to put these things into words helps our prayers and internal conversations focus on what is most important. When we can't articulate the significance of what happened, we often get stuck looping through the memories of the events. Even in our prayers we can feel more like a news reporter reciting to God what occurred than a child seeking comfort from a parent who understands. Transitioning from *angry grief* about what happened to *memorializing grief* for the good things lost allows us to engage in a more healing and restorative conversation with God.

This transition doesn't happen all at once, as we would prefer. It comes about like any other developmental process, gradually. And initially, memorializing-grief doesn't feel much better than angry grief. If anything, it feels more vulnerable.

But moving from an angry grief to a memorializing grief does begin to open a broader emotional and relational range of options. Anger is constrictive. The only options are overpower or power through. With grief, we experience more choices. We can let people in. We can be sad then focus on something else. We can appreciate the lessons hard times taught us. Grieving allows us to regain some emotional elasticity. As that happens, notice it, appreciate it, and be encouraged that you're moving in a good direction.

QUESTIONS FOR REFLECTION

1. How would you summarize the idea of interviewing or personifying your pain? How would you summarize the benefits that can come from it?

2. What did you learn about the *why* behind the *what* of your pain as you reflected on the questions in this chapter?

Chapter 8

WHAT HAPPENED?

Objectivity about painful experiences is difficult whether we are angry or grieving. But objectivity is what we will be after in this chapter. To this point, we have focused on gaining a fuller understanding of the personal significance of the events that hurt you. We focused on feeling understood.

The question to answer in this chapter is, What can I learn from these painful events? You won't have a definitive answer when you finish this chapter. Sometimes, we never get a completely satisfying answer. But we can begin to arrange the raw material of our stories in a way that helps us answer this question, to the degree that a satisfying answer exists.

We will again take a deeper dive into material you've already compiled. Review the Events and After time periods on your time line. Then review verses 9 to 22 of Psalm 44. The emotions the psalmist expresses in these verses likely mirror your own as you remember the painful events you experienced.

We will be looking again at these raw times, but our approach will be more objective and forensic than expressive. Here is what that means—and what it doesn't mean. If we misunderstand "objective" to mean value free, then it feels like we're being asked to overlook the wrongness of what happened. That would be infuriating. But objectivity doesn't mean we declare a bad situation to be less wrong; it means that we examine the situation *to learn* more than *to feel*.

If you feel a wave of defensiveness as you read that, pause. Don't be rushed. Take the time you need. Just because you are at this point in this book, doesn't mean you are at this point in your journey. It may be that you need to work on this section in several smaller increments. Be as patient with yourself as you would be with a friend on a comparable journey.

When we're done with this chapter, it should feel like you peeled the soundtrack away from a movie script. The script is what contains the facts of the movie: Who did what and when? What was said? Who said it? When were critical decisions made, who made them, and what did they know at the time? The soundtrack is what accentuates and builds the emotions to the script. We want to be able to evaluate the movie script of our painful experiences with less impact from the soundtrack.

We will seek to accomplish this by doing two things:

1. Identify critical junctures in our painful experiences.
2. Think well about how to allocate responsibility for our painful experiences.

CRITICAL JUNCTURES

A critical juncture is a point in our life story that results in significant changes. Sometimes we are aware that a critical juncture is occurring. For instance, when we decided about college or a first career, we knew these were moments that would impact the direction of our life. Other times, we are not aware a choice will be significant. For example, we may have gone to the library to study many times and not much came of it, but then one time we met the person who would become our spouse.

Don't get caught in the trap of thinking that just because something was a critical juncture, you should have seen it coming or known to do something different. That is a recipe for false guilt. Discerning how to think about our responsibility and others' responsibility in these critical junctures is the focus of the second part of this chapter.

First, we will explore six question clusters to discern what we might learn from our painful experience. There may not be answers to each question for every painful experience.

1. What are things I should have done differently?
   - Limit your answers to actions or responses that were morally wrong, not only ineffective.
   - These are things for which the appropriate response is repentance.
   - The best word for how you feel about these things is *guilt*.

2. What are things I wish I had done differently?
   - Limit your answers to things you could have reasonably known to do differently.
   - These are things for which the appropriate response is to grow wiser.
   - The best word for how you feel about these things is *regret*.

3. What are things I wish I had seen more clearly?
   - Limit your answers to things that could be known without the benefit of hindsight.

- These are things for which the appropriate response is to grow more situationally aware. For example, this might include acknowledgment of a loved one's addiction when there were adequate warning signs.
- As we grow more situationally aware, we lose childlike innocence. Learning to value a less innocent faith will become a major theme in the rest of our journey, especially chapter 16.

4. What are ways I was sinned against?
    - Limit your answers to actions that were morally wrong, not just personally offensive.
    - These are things for which the appropriate response from those who hurt you is repentance. Forgiving your offender may or may not result in the restoration of trust (see appendix 1 on page 158 for more on the relationship between forgiveness and trust).
    - From this question, you are seeking to grow more relationally wise.

5. What are ways or times my interests were neglected?
    - Limit your answers to forms of care that could realistically be foreseen without hindsight.
    - While these things may not have been sinful omissions by the people around you, they were hurtful. The appropriate response from the neglectful person(s) is an acknowledgment that their failure to fulfill this reasonable expectation was hurtful.
    - Such an acknowledgment begins to restore trust.

6. What are key moments that no one could foresee or change?
    - This is where painful moments go that do not fit any of the other categories.

- These are aspects of your experience that can only
  be grieved. There is no guilt to repent of, folly to
  learn from, or offense to mend.

After you complete your answers to these six questions, share them with a trusted friend, pastor, or counselor. These are "laundry-sorting questions." If answers
get in the wrong pile, like a red sock with your white
linens, the rest of the process is unlikely to be as effective
as you desire.

ALLOCATION OF RESPONSIBILITY

Now that you have your lists, it may be helpful to organize
them further. The chart below is meant to help you begin
to "see" what you or others can begin to "do" to process
or resolve your pain. You will notice there are three col-
umns. The first column represents areas where the active
response belongs to you. The second column represents
areas where the active response belongs to another person
(e.g., friend, family member, colleague). The final column
represents things over which only God had control.

The three rows represent the kind of responses that
would help you resolve the painful experience. The first
row includes actions that are morally wrong, so the individual who committed those actions should repent. The
second row includes actions that are foolish or short-
sighted, so the person learns.

The third row includes things that are "just hard," so
if a person was involved, they sympathetically acknowledge what happened. When an adverse circumstance is
purely a matter of God's providence, we grieve—with
God's compassion—that it happened. This protects us
from false guilt.

Take your answers to the six questions above and sort them into the categories on the responsibility allocation chart below.

	My Responsibility	Other Person	God's Providence
Guilt (Wrong)	I Repent Question Cluster 1	They Repent Question Cluster 4	
Regret (Foolish or Shortsighted)	I Learn Question Cluster 2	They Learn Question Cluster 5	
Just Painful (Hard but Not Bad or Foolish)	I Acknowledge Question Cluster 3	They Acknowledge Question Cluster 5 or 6	We Grieve Question Cluster 6

Filling out a chart such as this doesn't "fix" everything. But it can give us a sense of direction when we've felt stuck for a long time. Knowing the best-fit verbs (i.e., *repent*, *learn*, *acknowledge*, *grieve*) and who those verbs belong to, helps us identify what can be done with each of the hurts we've experienced.

QUESTIONS FOR REFLECTION

1. What did you learn from sorting key events from your painful experience using the six questions?

2. What did you learn from placing your answers to the six questions into the responsibility allocation chart?

Chapter 9

ANGRY WITH GOD BECAUSE OF GOD'S PEOPLE?

Identifying who we are angry with is important. But it is not always as easy to discern as we think it should be. Sometimes when we're angry, it feels like any target will do. But directing our anger at the wrong target serves as a distraction to reaching resolution.

It makes sense that being hurt by God's people can result in being upset with God. His people are supposed to be his ambassadors (2 Corinthians 5:20). If an American ambassador offends another country's leadership, it is as if the offense came from the United States itself. This reality is why Christians should take our actions with others seriously. As Christians, we carry God's reputation with us.

But to continue with the ambassador analogy, if the American ambassador offends the French ambassador, it would be unwise for the French ambassador to end their relationship with the United States. While such a move may be understandable, it would come at an unnecessary cost.

This is the kind of distinction we want to make in this reflection. In the same way we would not want to write off an entire country because of a bad ambassador, we don't want to turn our back on God because of a hurtful Christian or church. But what do we do? There are three actions we can take to make meaningful progress in the journey we've begun.

1. RECEIVE GOD'S COMPASSION

You don't have to prove to anyone that the hurtful things a Christian or a church did were wrong to receive God's compassion. His compassion is not mediated by the jury of his church. Yes, churches should represent God accurately, but like any other person or entity this side of heaven, they can fail to do so—sometimes in severely hurtful and downright evil ways.

Much of what stokes the fire of our angry grief is trying to prove to other Christians that our grief is legitimate. To the degree that it helps, I want to say I am sorry for how Christians have hurt you and how you have felt obligated to defend your grief. I hope that acknowledgment helps you settle into the next stages of the grieving process. (This book is about your journey toward a healthy and renewed relationship with God, so defining the consequences that may be warranted for those who hurt you is beyond the scope of this book. I do want to acknowledge that accountability and legal consequences for illegal actions are biblically legitimate responses.)

2. IDENTIFY SAFE CHRISTIAN FRIENDS

Think of friends who accurately reflect God's character as the "remnant" of God's people that is spoken of in the Old Testament (e.g., Ezra 9:8). They are a precious gift in difficult seasons. While thinking in these terms is not

meant to suggest that the majority of Christians are disin-
genuous, it may capture your experience.

You don't have to believe Christendom is a sham for
it to feel like these few, trusted Christian friends are the
remnant of God's care for you. We may find that, like
Elijah in 1 Kings 19, our pain has made our guesstimate
of the number of God's faithful people much bleaker than
it actually is. But even if this is the case, we begin our journey toward a healthier perspective from where we are.
God will care for us in that state of mind, as he did Elijah.

This would be a good time to go to those Christian
friends who have been faithfully walking alongside you
and say something like, "I want you to know I really
appreciate your friendship. I may not be in a great place
right now, but it would be a lot darker without you. You
have been a blessing in my life when I really needed it.
Thank you."

3. PACE PERSONAL AND RELATIONAL RECOVERY

If your anger is more with God's people than with God,
your journey may be a bit more complicated. Some things
are easier to process with people than with God; other
things are easier to process with God than with people.
Anger is one of those (see the Additional Resources
appendix on page 158 for more on this topic).

As you work through your relationship with God's
people who hurt you, you may need to take a few steps in
processing your hurt and anger before you can fruitfully
engage with them. And they may need to take a few steps
in acknowledging what happened before they can fruitfully engage with you.

Your work in the "What Was Good?" and "What Happened?" chapters may be helpful in assessing whether you are ready to engage. When you're ready, you could send your summary of those exercises to the individual(s) who hurt you with a note saying, "This is how I remember the things that happened—both the good parts of what we shared and what has led to the strain between us. If you think this is a good-faith effort at summarizing what happened, I would be interested in trying to restore some of our relationship."

Before sending a note like this, be aware that you need to have the emotional resilience to bear these individuals declining your invitation or stating that they do not find your summary reasonable. Until you are ready for the possibility of such a response, your work should be on personal recovery. But if you are ready to engage and they decline your invitation, you can rest in the knowledge that you have fulfilled the "as far as it depends on you" (Romans 12:18) phrase to try to live at peace with your fellow believers.

CONCLUSION

It would be easy for the culmination of this reflection to distract from its intent. The primary point of this chapter is not the question of when you are ready to extend an olive branch to someone who hurt you and whether they are willing to respond in kind. The primary point is to avoid the common tendency to allow anger from being hurt by God's people to be mistaken for anger at God.

We do not want the fallenness and fickleness of people to distract us from the trustworthiness of God. The reality is God's people do not always represent God well. If the people who bear his name hurt you and you pull away from God, the cost to you is severe. It is similar to when a country cuts off all imports, exports, and treaty protections from another country because of a rude ambassador. The encouragement of this chapter is to avoid cutting yourself off from all that God wants to be in your life because some of his people represent him in offensive or even abhorrent ways.

QUESTIONS FOR REFLECTION

1. Are your hurt and anger directed toward God or toward God's people? If you were to guess at percentages, what percentage of your pain do you attribute to God versus God's people?

2. If your anger toward God's people has leaked into your relationship with God, what effects of this cut-off-relationship-with-the-whole-country strategy have you begun to experience?

Chapter 10

WHAT MADE THE PAIN WORSE?

We are entering the final time period as we continue to explore the pain that prompted our angry grief. We first delved into the Before time period, which consisted of the events that were so good that the disruption of them was painful. Then we looked at the During and some of the After period, when the painful events occurred that marred what was good. Now, we will focus on the After, when subsequent experiences added to your pain, even if they were not necessarily tied to the original disruptive events.

By way of example, let's consider the painful case of adultery. Here is how we might break down the central events and the circumstances surrounding them into the time periods we have been discussing:

- *Before*: This is every part of the dating, engagement, and marriage that was good.
- *During*: This includes the compromises, cover-ups, and unfaithfulness of the adultery.
- *After*: These are the things that occur after the affair is discovered that add to the pain—things

like blame shifting, partial truth telling, or apathy toward restoration.

Too often, as we try to process the past, the After period either gets neglected or lumped into the During. If it gets neglected, then it meets the same icy silence that makes God seem distant from our pain. If it gets lumped into the During, then we misinterpret many of the people, actions, and events—everything is earthquake; nothing is aftershock.

To prevent neglecting the unique pain of this time period, we will continue to interview our pain. We will consider five question clusters. Like before, not every factor will fit every experience of suffering. Reflect on the ones that fit your experience and ignore those that do not.

1. AFTERSHOCKS OF SUFFERING

Painful experiences often have aftershocks. Aftershocks may be emotional. Betrayals bruise trust, so we may begin viewing even healthy relationships with suspicion. Suffering resulting in shame leaves us feeling stigmatized or defiled. Other aftershocks are logistical. Perhaps the painful events we went through hurt us financially, and we find ourselves needing to say no to loved ones regarding things we desperately want to say yes to.

A near-universal aftershock of suffering is emotional fatigue; we just don't have the emotional energy to process other life challenges that come our way. We begin to avoid things that need our attention, or we make easy but unwise choices even when we know the long-term consequences will be worse, just because we can't handle making the hard but better choice.

Here are questions to help you identify aftershocks of your initial painful events.

- What did you neglect as a result of the aftershocks of your suffering? What are the implications?
- What emotions were dominant during that time? How do they interfere with life now?
- How was trust damaged during your suffering? What current good relationships are adversely affected by this generalized lack of trust?
- If you were young, what age-appropriate life skills did you not learn during your suffering? How does the underdevelopment of those skills affect you now?
- If you were an adult, what good memories do you look back on with a tinge of pain? What events in the life of your children or grandchildren were disrupted?

Remember, God has the same compassion toward you when you struggle with these aftershocks as he did when you experienced the initial climactic event(s). For your flourishing, God wants to see you grow to be less affected by these aftershocks, but he is not rushing you. God does not view you as being "behind" or "deficient" because of these challenges. God knows your story. He understands why these things are hard or delayed. As a good father, he takes extra delight in your progress because he knows what you are overcoming.

2. COINCIDING SUFFERING

Not every hardship after a painful experience is an aftershock. Sometimes multiple experiences of suffering just coincide during the same season of life. A family may experience a house fire then, a month later, a job loss because of a down economy. The fire and the job loss are unrelated; they just happened around the same time.

Even when there is not a cause-and-effect relationship with your initial suffering, these hardships add to the emotional weight and logistical difficulty. Our thinking can take on a superstitious quality as we feel "cursed." We embrace this superstitious thinking to try to make meaning of the multiple hardships. Feeling cursed makes us ask by whom, and this again misdirects our anger toward God.

But this way of making meaning is no more accurate than me getting upset with my wife because she happened to walk into the room at the same moment I missed a nail and hit my thumb. There is a correlation in time between the events but no causal relationship. My misguided meaning-making only creates distance in a relationship that could be a source of comfort.

Here are questions to help you differentiate whether suffering is an aftershock or coincidental.

- Is it likely this later hardship would have happened regardless of the earlier event(s)?
- Did you have this aptitude weakness (e.g., hard time focusing) or emotional vulnerability prior to the painful event(s)?
- Was this challenge that arose in the After period normal for the season of life you were/are in?

Even if you determine that certain hardships you have faced are coincidental, they still "count." They're still hardships. God does not ignore coincidental challenges; he cares for you in the midst of them.

But for how we make sense of our life story, it is helpful if we keep them narratively separate. Yes, my wife walked in the room. Yes, I hit my thumb with the hammer. Yes, it hurt like the dickens. But for my marriage narrative to be accurate, I need to keep these two things narratively separate—my wife didn't make me hit my thumb. I hurt our relationship by conflating the two. The same can happen in our relationship with God.

3. DRY QUIET TIMES AND PRAYER

Emotionally loud experiences tend to drown out emotionally quieter experiences. If I am feeling the pain of a broken leg, my ability to enjoy a flourless dark chocolate torte (the best of all possible desserts) will be diminished. The cake tastes the same—however, my senses are saturated and distracted. This same principle holds true in our relationship with God.

When the painful experiences of life are emotionally loud, they can dull our ability to enjoy our relationship with God. God is the same as he has always been. He is every bit as much for us and with us. But our pain inhibits our capacity to take solace in God.

Think of it this way: We need to learn to appreciate God's presence like a person exhausted by chemotherapy appreciates the presence of a spouse or parent in their hospital room. The suffering may significantly limit how meaningfully this person can engage their loved ones. But the muted ability to enjoy their family's presence does not diminish how much the relationship is valued.

If you feel that your ability to get comfort from your relationship with God has been dulled, if your quiet times and prayer life are dry, here are a few suggestions to help you begin to regain an appreciation of God's presence.

- Allow simple "thank you" prayers to be enough when you are tired.
- Listen to the Bible rather than read it. This takes less mental energy and concentration.
- When you hear one meaningful truth that resonates with you, pause, and savor it. That may be all you can take in that day.
- Through the spiritual discipline of silence, imagine God sitting patiently with you like a family member in the hospital room.

These things won't make a dry quiet time burst forth with vibrancy. But if they help dryness not get mistaken for God's absence, then they will have accomplished something significant.

4. CLUMSY FRIENDS

In the chapter on the During time period, we focused more on people whom you considered friends but who did things that were hurtful. In the After time period, we want to recognize and curb the tendency to interpret anything that is upsetting or disappointing as malicious.

Here we are looking at things a friend may have done that unintentionally made your pain worse. Perhaps a friend asked an excited question about your baby at an office party, not knowing about your miscarriage. Maybe a friend tried to be encouraging, but in their attempt, they were insensitive to your pain. For a variety of reasons, those around us are often emotionally clumsy when we're hurting.

The fact that their clumsiness was unintentional doesn't mean it was not hurtful. Our goal here is to learn to distinguish safe pain from unsafe pain—distinguish safe people, who at times are clumsy in their care, from malicious people, who try to convince us their self-serving actions were for our good. Without this ability, we begin to avoid genuinely caring people, and this fosters a sense of isolation that makes it easier to believe that nobody— including God—cares about us.

To help you discern whether your friends were being intentionally hurtful or just emotionally or relationally clumsy, consider these questions:

- What did your friend know at the time of the interaction?
- In their mind, what was the desired effect of their words or actions? If you're not sure, consider asking them.
- Has it been like your friend to be malicious in the way your fear or pain interprets their actions?

If there is reason to believe that your friend was well-intended but clumsy, consider having a conversation such as this: "I don't think you were trying to be hurtful, but when you said/did [blank], it made this difficult time harder for me. I value our friendship. It would help me resist the urge to isolate if you understood why it was hurtful and would work on not saying/doing things like that again." While these can be hard conversations, we want to weigh their awkwardness against the pain of unnecessary isolation.

5. CONSEQUENCES OF REACTIONARY CHOICES

The After period can also get worse because of unwise or destructive choices we make. Chapter 14 will focus more on the poor choices we can make when we're hurting. For now, we want to acknowledge that while suffering may have been at the forefront of the experience, we can still make sinful or foolish choices in response to our pain.

Consider the person who, after a major grief event, seeks escape through alcohol to such a degree that their drinking becomes addictive. Or the spouse betrayed by adultery who shares too much information with a coworker and sparks an emotional affair. After suffering, our choices can make a bad situation worse. This doesn't make the initial tragedy our fault, but we do need to own anything we added to the problem.

When we fail to see our contribution (when it exists) to the aftermath of a bad situation, we take on a mentality of powerlessness. We fall into the mindset that because there was *nothing we could do* (past tense) to prevent the initial tragedy that there is now *nothing we can do* (present tense) to make things better. Succumbing to a powerless mindset makes our angry grief worse.

To help you discern what impact your choices had on the aftermath of your painful experience, consider these questions.

- What things have I done that I would consider wrong if someone else did them?
- What things have I done that I would consider foolish if someone else did them?
- What things have trusted friends cautioned me about, but I've resisted heeding their concerns?
- Which of my After time period actions would I undo if I could?

The value of identifying our mistakes is twofold. First, it alleviates a sense of powerlessness. Identifying these actions helps you see that you can make choices that meaningfully affect your life. Second, it protects your life from a moral drift. Many people can look back on a painful experience as a time when their decision-making deteriorated and life declined dramatically. This awareness is a protection against that process.

Your goal in this chapter has been to differentiate the damage done by the earthquake from damage perhaps still being done by the aftershocks. We couldn't prevent the earthquake itself. But we know that major earthquakes are followed by aftershocks, and we can prepare and respond in wise ways. Making this distinction helps us see we are not as powerless as we fear.

QUESTIONS FOR REFLECTION

1. Has it been your tendency to neglect the After time period or lump it in with the During time period?

2. Which of the five factors that influence the After time period have affected you the most?

SECTION 3: ALLEVIATING THE EFFECTS OF PAIN

Angry grief creates more than an emotional disruption. Our emotions are certainly involved and important. But the mental, social, volitional, and spiritual disruptions we experience require us to understand that more than just our emotions are involved.

Section 3 will focus the effects of angry grief on five areas of our lives: emotions, thoughts, relationships, choices, and view of God. My hope is that working through this section will provide three benefits: (1) validation that your painful experiences are real and important; (2) words to articulate ways they have impacted your life; and (3) guidance on how to reduce the disruption they cause you now.

Chapter 11

THE EFFECTS
ON OUR EMOTIONS

So far in this book we have sought to establish a safe context to process our angry grief (section 1) and to put our experience into words so we can process our pain (section 2). Now we are entering a new phase. We want to offset the various disruptions angry grief brings into our life. We will start by seeking to understand and respond to the emotional disruptions.

As we try to understand what occurs when we get stuck in the angry phase of grief, it can be helpful to differentiate primary and secondary emotions.

- Primary emotions are how we feel about an event, experience, or situation.
- Secondary emotions are how we feel about our primary emotions.

A COMMON EXAMPLE

Let's take a common case study. Imagine a parent playing with their children in the yard. One of the children begins to move toward a busy street. How does the parent feel about the situation where their child is at risk? Afraid. That is their primary emotion. How does the parent feel

about being afraid for their child's safety? Angry. That is
their secondary emotion.

This brief vignette helps illustrate several distinctions
between primary and secondary emotions.

- Primary emotions tend to be our more vulnerable
  emotions.
- Secondary emotions tend be stronger, self-protective
  emotions.
- Primary emotions are often less obvious to onlookers.
- Secondary emotions get the attention.
- When people focus on our primary emotions, we feel
  cared for and understood.
- When people focus on our secondary emotions, we
  feel judged and misunderstood.

Let's return to our case study. If you asked the child
intercepted from the busy street, "At this moment, do you
think your parent is angry or afraid?" chances are, the child
would respond, "angry," because the tone and volume of
the parent's secondary emotion would have come through
as they yelled, "Stop!"

If you confronted the parent for being angry, the parent
would get indignant. "What am I supposed to do, just let
them run in the street? Am I supposed to stay calm when my
child is in danger?" However, if you said, "I know it's scary
for your child to be in danger, but they're safe now. Take a
deep breath," you could deliver the same message—relax—
and get a much more receptive response.

USING THIS DISTINCTION

Now let's move on from the simplicity of this case study
to the question, How does this distinction help us navigate angry grief? The answer begins with the realization

that our secondary emotion, anger, feels safer than our primary emotion, grief. When we're hurt, we want to feel safer. But relying on our secondary emotions pushes people, and God, away (it at least impairs our ability to receive the care God wants to offer).

Our initial task is to talk about our experience while staying grounded in our primary emotions. To illustrate what this means, imagine drawing a house with a tree on one side. Imagine drawing that picture with a red crayon. Now, imagine drawing the same picture with a gray crayon. We can draw the same picture with different colors.

Similarly, we can tell the same story in the tone of different emotions. The red crayon represents anger, and the gray crayon represents grief. Your goal here is to tell the story you collated in section 2 in gray instead of red. We've taken the time to collate the story and validate the red so that telling the story in gray doesn't feel like mini-mizing what happened.

The natural question is, What is this new way of tell-ing the story like? Telling the story in gray impacts the moments when your voice gets louder, your throat gets tight, or your eyes get sharp as you talk. These responses aren't bad, but they indicate that you're putting down the gray crayon and picking up the red one. These "fight responses" reveal the moments when you want to focus on staying in your primary emotions. You want to express the disruption you felt in those moments rather than trying to prove a point.

Here are a few examples that illustrate a shift from talking in red to talking in gray:

- Instead of asking, "Can you believe that in all of this, not one person called me?!" you might say,

"What was hurtful was that I kept waiting for someone to reach out to me and no one did."

- Instead of saying, "Right then and there I knew no one in that group cared about anything I had to say," you might say, "When what I said couldn't be restated back to me any clearer than it was, it became apparent something was more important than how these things impacted me."
- Instead of saying, "I was done with it. All of it. It was all a sham, and I was done playing the game," you might say, "That's when I realized I had to pull back. I wasn't on the same page with people I thought were on the same team. I realized doing more or trying harder would only make things worse."

These contrasting statements model four principles for how to tell your story in gray—that is, with your primary emotions in the foreground.

First, you will notice more "I statements" than "you statements." This is particularly important when you are talking to someone who hurt you. When you are talking to another person, "you statements" are more confrontational, while "I statements" focus on personal experience.

Second, rhetorical questions turn into statements of feeling, as in the first example. This makes what you are saying feel more like a request for compassion and less like the closing argument in a trial.

Third, the alternative versions restate mind-reading declaratives (statements that presume you know other people's motives) into a summary of the conclusion you drew from the situation. This moves you out of the role of "all knowing voice from above" to the role of a hurting person within the story.

Fourth, the alternative versions remove the dramatic flair. They are vulnerable and factual rather than powerful or theatrical. Again, it is not that the flair is bad. It's that the flair is ineffective for what you want to accomplish—inviting others into your experience in a meaningful way.

These changes are helpful to the person hearing you—and they are good for you too. They help the person hearing you enter your story. Your focus on primary emotions elicits compassion. It draws people in. And it helps you, partly because it draws your friend in but also because it places you in a better frame of mind to receive their comfort. Your guard is down, in a good way.

To summarize, when we get stuck in the anger phase of grief, one way this manifests is that we become too reliant on our secondary emotions to express how we feel. Secondary emotions push people away and leave us alone in our pain. We are at a place in our journey where we want to begin telling our story in gray. We want to progress in our grief and speak in a way that invites the comfort we long to receive.

QUESTIONS FOR REFLECTION

1. Now that you understand the difference between primary and secondary emotions, consider this question: how much do you rely on secondary emotions to express hurt and pain?

2. Which of the communication suggestions for telling your story in gray will be most important for you to begin communicating in your primary emotions?

Chapter 12

THE EFFECTS ON OUR THOUGHTS

Anger is an emotion that usually comes with cognitive content. By contrast, sometimes when we're depressed and someone asks, "What are you thinking about when you feel these things?" we honestly reply, "I don't know. I just feel down." But with anger, our thoughts usually have content: events we replay, phrases we repeat, or arguments we're still trying to win.

This makes sense because anger is, perhaps, the most moral emotion. Anger declares things wrong and doesn't feel like it can subside until these wrongs are made right. Because of this, when grief stagnates in the anger phase, our cognitive world gets set on repeat. Even when we're tired of being angry, we're not sure how to silence our thoughts until the disruption that prompted our anger is resolved.

The churchy answers to this dilemma often only add fuel to the fire of our anger. "Everything may not be made right in this world, but you can rest knowing it will be in heaven." That feels like telling a starving person about the incredible buffet in heaven's cafeteria. "Because Jesus suffered an injustice far greater than our own, we really shouldn't focus on our own injustices." That feels like we're being silenced by the one who's supposed to be our source of comfort.

The problem with these responses is that they try to tell us why we shouldn't feel the way we do (or, at best, why we should ignore what we feel) instead of helping us process our pain. That approach adds another layer of unfairness to the anger we're already grappling with.

In contrast, our earlier work in this journey should reassure us that Scripture does not ignore our pain, and God is more compassionately engaged with our cognitive disruptions than these responses suggest. And so, we will seek to honor God's engagement by alleviating the cognitive disruptions in two ways: first, making the sticky thoughts less sticky, and second, concluding the perpetual trial in our mind.

ADDRESSING STICKY THOUGHTS

Anger tends to be repetitive. That means you can make a list of the things you say to yourself in your anger. Perhaps it's something like this.

- "I'm done!"
- "It's all fake!"
- "It was all for nothing!"
- "Forget it all!"
- "Nobody cares!"

These may not be your phrases, but you know the things that have been stuck on loop in your mind. When you say these things, the energy and despair of your past pain infuses the present moment.

Part of managing the cognitive interference of grief-stagnated-in-anger is learning to engage these thoughts differently by, first, recognizing the feelings behind the words. The distinction between primary and secondary emotions can again be helpful. When a sticky thought intrudes, remind yourself, "This is hot grief. It's okay to be hurt. It's okay to be sad." Hopefully, this reminder will allow you to embrace more of God's compassion and, thereby, alleviate some of the fighting mode you retreat into when you feel compelled to prove your pain is valid.

Second, replace the phrase with a temporal description rather than a universal declaration. You might change your phrase like this:

- "I'm done!" becomes "I'm tired."
- "It's all fake!" becomes "Things aren't as simple and clear as I thought they were."
- "It was all for nothing!" becomes "My dream for this situation isn't going to come true."
- "Forget it all!" becomes "It hurts to remember."
- "Nobody cares!" becomes "I'm sad that they don't seem to get it."

"I'm tired" is more temporal than "I'm done." "Things aren't as simple as I thought they were" isn't as final as "It's all fake." "It hurts to remember" describes your experience in this moment, while "Forget it all" is a desperate statement that is impossible to follow through on.

None of these new phrases dismisses your grief. Instead, they focus on what is sad rather than what makes you mad. Your goal is to progress in grief rather than just stop being angry. Replace your angry phrases with words that give direction to your grief.

Third, engage with the implication of the restated phrase by asking a question (the list below corresponds to the bulleted lists above):

- What would it look like for me to rest, emotionally and physically?
- What are the tensions that I didn't see before but need to manage now?
- What redemptive things did/could occur, even though my main dream for this situation did not?
- Can I give myself permission to stop rehearsing what happened?
- Who are the people who have understood and supported me?

These aren't the only alternative questions, but they are meant to provide examples of the style of question you can ask to disrupt the repetition of sticky thoughts. The goal is to give yourself the freedom to feel your primary emotions and, thereby, provide more fruitful questions for your mind to ponder. You aren't eliminating emotions and thoughts; you are getting them unstuck by giving them direction.

BRINGING THE TRIAL TO CONCLUSION

The narration of how things should have been handled, or what we would like to have said to prove our case can be even stickier than the short phrases above. We can get completely wrapped up in rewriting and replaying different versions of these fantasy events.

As you seek to bring this mental trial to an end, ask yourself a few questions.

- Who is present at my mental trial? Why is each person there?
- What is the point I am trying to make? What is the false point I don't want people to believe?
- If the trial was resolved the way I wanted, what would be different?

These questions can help you end your cognitive court proceeding in three ways.

1. *Change your audience.* Too often we focus on changing the mind of the defendant in our trial— that is, the person(s) who hurt or offended us. Instead, who are the current people from this situation who are meaningfully involved in your life? In real life, rather than in your mind, is it possible to have a conversation with them?

2. *Clarify your message.* Too often we focus on declaring the hurtful things bad. Instead, what are the things that you want the safe people in your life to understand aren't true? How can you articulate your fears in such a way that key people can comfort them or help you refute them?

3. *Request changes.* Too often we focus on getting an admission of guilt or neglect. Instead, what would create a context where you felt safe, honored, or cared for? With those who are concerned enough to be trusted, share these things to begin establishing a social environment that allows you to cognitively rest.

Again, these categories will fit some hurts more than others. Allow these examples to be a prompt to a healthier style of thinking. The healthy outcome of anger is resolution. Although we are rarely able to eliminate the influence of the painful event, we can gain a sense that the future will be less marred by past wrongs.

CONCLUSION

What you have now are strategies. That is different from having victory or resolution. Because you have an approach, it can be easy to think that the issue is resolved. That is overly optimistic, such as the athlete who thinks that because he has the drills, the skill should already be achieved.

We have discussed approaches to handling the cognitive interference of angry grief, and now we begin the process of becoming skilled at using these approaches and tailoring them to the pain that prompted our angry grief. Give yourself the freedom to practice these strategies and understand that relief will build as you become more proficient in them.

QUESTIONS FOR REFLECTION

1. How do you feel about the possibility of sharing with a trusted friend the more vulnerable expressions of your sticky-angry thoughts, those that focus on your primary emotions?

2. What was the key message you wanted to convey in the mental trials that you rehearsed? What would it mean to have someone understand and sympathize with that message?

Chapter 13

THE EFFECTS ON OUR RELATIONSHIPS

You may have heard people say, "Anger is divisive." This is true. But it is true in more ways than we often realize. Typically, when we say, "Anger is divisive," we mean that our angry words or actions offend other people and, thereby, harm our relationship with them. This is the way anger is *interpersonally divisive*—that is, it creates division between people.

But anger is also *intrapersonally divisive*; that is, anger causes us to sort people into groups in our mind. When we are angry, we reflexively divide people into groups: (a) good people and bad people, (b) safe people and unsafe people, or (c) people who "get it" and people who don't. Because our pain makes us wary, the first groups are small, and the second groups are large.

We may think that if we don't talk about how we divide people, then it doesn't hurt anyone. But dividing people in our minds hurts us. Living in a highly "teamed" world is unhealthy for our soul. Having suspicion as our default disposition can keep casual relationships from developing into deeper friendships. Even if we're nice, people can tell when we're guarded. When we are less authentic, so are the people around us. This inauthenticity keeps relationships shallow.

Socially, as we seek to get unstuck from the grief-as-anger phase, we want to remove the mindset that says, "If I don't *know* you're for me, then I *assume* you're against me." For a time, this mindset may have kept us safe. But if it calcifies into a life principle, it becomes a lens of suspicion that traps us in a world defined by our pain.

FROM UNIFORMS TO SPECTRUM AND QUADRANTS

Our first goal is to move people from wearing uniforms—being *either* allies *or* adversaries—to being accurately located across a spectrum. Actually, there are at least two spectrums that are helpful to consider as we seek to reduce the artificial teaming in how we think about people.

The chart below is meant to help you gauge your level of trust for people. Once you familiarize yourself with how the two spectrums form four quadrants, you can plot relationships—with dots—that represent where you assign the various people in your life, and then ask yourself whether that is where they belong.

		How well I know you	
Trust	**Q1** Pleasant, Casual Relationships		**Q4** Trusted, Meaningful Relationships
		How much you impact my life	
Mistrust	Casual Relationships with Unnecessary Mistrust **Q2**		Wisely, Mistrusted Relationships **Q3**
	Little Impact		**Much Impact**

Spectrum 1 (Vertical Axis): Trust and How Well I Know You. Our goal is to elevate the starting point for new, casual relationships from negative (below the dotted line) to neutral. Past pain has a way of plotting new relationships lower on the scale toward mistrust. This requires potential friends to pay the trust debt created by hurtful friends.

Spectrum 2 (Horizontal Axis): How Much You Impact My Life. Wisdom says, the more you impact my life, the better I need to know you before I trust you. We need to know a business partner better than a gym friend because the impact they have on our life is greater. We want to begin to let wisdom, rather than suspicion rooted in past pain, determine how much we trust the people in our lives.

These two spectrums make the four quadrants:

Q1 – Low Impact; Moderate Trust. This quadrant is for casual relationships. Because their impact on our life is relatively small, the degree of trust they need to "prove" should also be small. We want this to become the default quadrant for new relationships. This quadrant is where we look for future Q4 friends.

Q2 – Low Impact; Low Trust. This is the quadrant we are trying to depopulate. A significant percentage of these people should be in Q1, but because of our pain, this quadrant gets overpopulated.

Q3 – High Impact (Negative); Low Trust. This is the quadrant for unrepentant people who were part of the experience(s) that prompted this journey. These are people in whom it would be foolish to trust again.

Q4 – High Impact (Positive); High Trust. This is the quadrant we want to increase; it contains our most life-giving relationships. Early in this journey you were encouraged to confide in a few trusted friends. These are Q4 people. But we don't just want support network people in Q4. Being able to have meaningful relationships with people who aren't intimately aware of what happened is part of decentralizing these events from your life story.

Now, let's ask two questions: (1) How many people do you have in each quadrant? (2) How many potential Q4 people do you currently have in Q1 and Q2? Your step of faith for this chapter is to begin moving Q2 people to Q1 and Q1 people to Q4.

DESENSITIZING "GOD LANGUAGE"

Being on this journey means you are a person of faith and that your faith is important to you. That means casual Q1 relationships with people of faith may be a double-edged sword—candidates for becoming trusted Q4 friends but also individuals who may inadvertently talk in a way that exacerbates your past pain. Being aware of this dynamic can help you respond to it wisely.

We talk about things differently in casual conversations than in relationships where we know each other better. In school, we might talk about studying for a test as "no big deal" in one setting but with more care when we know our friend needs to do well to pass the class. Similarly, we talk about a meal differently in a casual setting than with a friend we know is working hard to lose weight.

This isn't duplicity. It is heightened care based on deeper awareness. But this is the dynamic that can lead us to unnecessarily banish many Q1 people to the mistrust quadrants, Q2 and Q3. Someone makes a casual comment about the goodness of God, the value of faith, or the beauty of community, and we reflexively become like the student grinding to pass a class who heard a classmate say they're not worried about the test at all. These are the moments we need to learn to respond to differently if we're going to make it possible for fellow Christians, especially those who don't know us well, to move from Q1 to Q4.

We start by realizing that casual statements of faith are not bad—that is, not rude or heretical; they're just incomplete and without context. While we are stagnated in the angry phase of grief, our pain provides the artificial context for every faith statement we hear. This is understandable, but it's not fair to our casual Q1 and Q2 friends. We want to honor the context in which they understood themselves to be speaking, rather than filtering their words through our pain, which they are likely unaware of.

If we're with a friend at sunset and they say, "Isn't everything God does amazing and beautiful?" that statement may set off alarms for us in light of our history. God has done—or, at least, allowed—some things in our life that weren't amazing or beautiful. But our friend was just commenting on the sunset. We don't want to douse their awe at God's creation.

In such a situation, we have three options for how to respond in a healthy way. The response we choose depends on our history with the person and our hopes for the future of that relationship.

1. Take our friend's statement as they meant it and affirm what they intended to affirm without trying to extrapolate what they would say about our situation. This approach is usually best for

people new to Q1 or those we don't anticipate moving toward Q4 soon.

2. In general terms—that is, without mentioning your personal history—ask your friend how they balance their statement with harsh realities we see in the world around us. This approach is helpful for people who are midway across Q1 and who we believe have potential to become Q4 friends.

3. Affirm what our friend intended to affirm and confide what makes their statement hard for us. This approach is, in effect, an invitation for a friend to move from Q1 to Q4.

You can begin to see how these options demonstrate the benefits of thinking of relationships on a spectrum rather than safe or unsafe. It gives you more options for how to respond to casual statements about God and faith than the all-or-nothing responses that arise from your pain. This more nuanced mindset will allow new relationships to grow at a healthier and more natural pace.

QUESTIONS FOR REFLECTION

1. What are ways that you've noticed your anger or hurt leading you to divide the people in your world into teams: safe and unsafe, get it and don't get it?

2. Who are the people who are midway or further across the Q1 quadrant who show good Q4 potential? What is the next step of trust you might take with them?

Chapter 14

THE EFFECTS
ON OUR CHOICES

On our journey together, we are learning many things about anger. Another observation about anger is that it doesn't rest well. Anger ties into the adrenal system. It energizes us. It calls for action. Anger and stillness coexist like caffeine and sleep.

This means that when we're angry, we are likely to be artificially active. This drive to be active can lead to great disruption. When we are angry, we're prone to react quickly and make choices without giving them due thought. So, we frequently look back on our choices with regret.

Understandably, we tend to get defensive about the bad choices we make during angry grief. We want to excuse them because of our pain. It feels as if anyone who questions our choices is invalidating the pain that prompted our anger. But the reality is that destructive choices made because of legitimate past pain are still destructive.

This cycle of harmful choices and defensiveness disrupts a healthy processing of grief. The negative consequences of our reactive choices distract us from our grief, and our defensiveness about our choices reinforces our anger. It can be a vicious cycle.

Our goal now is to learn to become less reactive with our choices when we're angry, not simply to be better decision makers but to further facilitate getting unstuck from the anger phase of grief.

As an example, consider a teenager who loses a parent. The teenager gets stuck in the anger phase of grief and begins to make reactionary choices. School doesn't seem "worth it" anymore, so they quit studying. Life seems unfair, so experimenting with drugs doesn't seem like a big deal. As the consequences for these choices mount, the teenager becomes defensive, "All you care about is what I do; not what I've been through." The reactive choices and their consequences become a distraction from processing grief and engaging life in ways that could be enjoyable.

The question is, How do we, in our angry grief, respond like this teenager? Once again, our discussion of primary and secondary emotions can be helpful. Unhealthy, reactionary choices emanate from our secondary emotions. Healthy, constructive choices emerge from our primary emotions. This distinction helps us navigate the misunderstanding that we're being asked to be passive. *The opposite of destructive choices is not passivity but action rooted in our primary emotions.*

Positively stated, our question becomes, If my angry grief influenced my decision-making less, how would my choices be different?" We'll use three sub-questions to help us answer this primary question.

1. What have I stopped doing that was healthy and life-giving?
2. What have I started doing that is unhealthy or wrong?
3. What do I respond to differently than I did before my painful experience?

WHAT HAVE I STOPPED DOING?

These are choices you may not even notice yourself making. We don't always pay attention to things in our life that fade away. Here are areas we commonly neglect when life is difficult.

- Life Management
  - Did you quit planning your day, week, or month?
  - Did you quit dreaming about the future and pursuing personal aspirations?

- Spiritual Development
  - Has your enjoyment of reading the Bible and Christian books faded?
  - Has your prayer life evaporated or become rote?

- Personal Interest
  - What hobbies or forms of expression (e.g., playing music) have you pulled away from?
  - Have you lost a sense of curiosity about life and people?

These questions reveal passive, nonchoices we frequently fall into that cause our world to fade into a lifeless gray. When stagnated grief results in life becoming perpetually gray, the splashes of red anger may be a welcome relief. Reengaging these healthy actions is a way to reintroduce color into our world.

As you reengage these activities, you may not get the full enjoyment at first. Imagine the feeling you get when you sleep on your arm wrong, and it loses circulation. As the blood returns, there is a prickly pain. That is not bad. It is part of the body's healthy response to correcting the absence of needed blood flow. Similarly, as you reengage, you may again experience the grief that stagnated when they dissipated.

The emotional equivalent of the tingly-arm effect is not permanent. Be patient with yourself as you reengage these life-giving activities. Allow the enjoyment of them you once knew to thaw.

WHAT HAVE I STARTED DOING?

You probably did notice yourself making other choices. At first, you were likely concerned about what you were doing, and your conscience felt guilty. When this happens, we often weigh our guilt against our pain and conclude that guilt is the lesser problem, so we give ourselves a pass.

These are some types of choices your anger may have contributed to.

- Escape/Numbing Choices
  - Pain is painful. It hurts. The actions in this category are attempts to keep from feeling pain. Have you begun to use drugs or alcohol to mask your pain?
  - Have you overengaged work or escaped through pornography to avoid your pain?

- Active-Defiant Choices
  - Have you increased high-risk choices such as gambling, overspending, or pushing moral lines?
  - Have you pushed away people or responsibilities?

- Judgmental Choices
  - Have you begun to assume the worst about other people's actions?
  - Do you find that "Yeah, but . . ." is your default response to pleasant events?

Metaphorically, think of these choices as cancer and the initial pain as a heart attack. It would be wise to treat the heart attack first. The imminence of the threat makes this obvious. But, if after treatment for the heart attack, you refused to get treatment for cancer, that would be foolish. This is the logic we want to apply to our decision-making process. The same anger that railed against the painful events that disrupted your life should also want to change these destructive choices.

By reversing these choices, you are showing that you care about the life that was disrupted by the pain that prompted your anger. *Allowing yourself to care again is a part of healthy grief.* When we lose a loved one, it is natural in our grief to wonder if it's worth getting close to others. But, in healthy grief, we conclude the answer is "Yes, it is," and our life is better because of it. That is what we're after here.

WHAT DO I RESPOND TO DIFFERENTLY?

These choices may not even feel like choices. Our reactions often feel as if they are happening to us more than they are coming from us, like reflexes. To the degree that the painful events that prompted this journey were traumatic, there may be some truth to this; in this case, it might be wise to consider counseling (see appendix 1 on page 158 for more resources on trauma and finding a counselor). Either way, the goal is to begin to regain control over our reactions.

Let's examine some arenas where you may be responding differently.

- People
  - Are there specific individuals who prompt you toward unhealthy or immoral choices?

- Are there groups of people or people in certain roles who prompt you toward unhealthy or immoral choices?

- Places
  - Are there specific locations that prompt you toward unhealthy or immoral choices?
  - Are there types of atmospheres (quiet places, chaotic places, etc.) that prompt you toward unhealthy or immoral choices?

- Activities
  - Are there specific activities that prompt you toward unhealthy or immoral choices?
  - Are there types of requests that prompt you toward unhealthy or immoral choices?

Reactions, by definition, require forethought to change; in the absence of forethought and preparation, reactions "just happen." If your reaction to seeing a roach is to hyperventilate, then without forethought that is what you will do. But if you mentally prepare for the occasion, you can maintain your composure and (hopefully) squash the vile intruder.

That is what we're after here. *We want to be sympathetic toward our reaction*. It is prompted by a painful experience. *But we also want to be intentional toward our reaction*. It is diminishing our quality of life. You don't have to be harsh with yourself to prepare for a healthier response to the reactions you listed above.

The variety in our possible reactions is too great to be as concrete as we would like at this point. But, if we consider the roach example, we identify a basic strategy.

1. Identify the prompt for our reaction: roach.
2. Name the types of reactions we have to the prompt: hyperventilation.
3. Identify approaches that mitigate these reactions: breathing exercises.
4. Mentally rehearse engaging the prompt with healthier responses.
5. Give yourself grace to grow in your response over time.

CHOOSING TO GRIEVE

Oh, that we could simply choose to grieve, as if it were as simple as starting a dishwasher and letting it run. Grief is not that simple. But our choices do impact our freedom to grieve.

In this respect, grief is similar to sleep; we cannot simply choose to sleep, but the choices we make impact the ease with which we fall asleep. What we have tried to do in this chapter is strategically identify the pivotal choices we have made, the contexts of those choices, and alternative choices that help get our grief unstuck from the anger phase.

Our goal has been more than reengage healthy habits, stop unhealthy habits, and be strategic about reactions. Yes, we have outlined those basic steps, but we did so for a larger reason. These things reinforced a lifestyle of avoiding grief. They reinforced a lifestyle of numbing, escaping, and reacting.

Returning to the parallel between grief and sleep, these things are like day naps or afternoon caffeine. They interfere with sleep. If our goal is sleep, we remove them to make our primary goal—a good night's sleep—more natural. Removing the interferences invites the natural-but-involuntary process (sleep or grief) to occur.

As you finish this chapter, your primary takeaway should be, "My choices matter." When we are trying to grieve well, this is a hope-filled statement. Because we can't start or stop grief like we open or close our eyes, it is easy to feel powerless. Identifying choices we can make to healthfully engage the grief process alleviates this feeling of powerlessness.

QUESTIONS FOR REFLECTION

1. How did the example of the teenager unhealthfully grieving the loss of a parent help you see defensiveness you may have regarding your grief-stagnated-in-anger and how it expresses itself?

2. This chapter asked three main questions to try to get at the way grief-induced anger has influenced your choices. Which of these questions are the most profitable for you to think through in order to begin to change unhealthy patterns?

Chapter 15

THE EFFECTS
ON OUR VIEW OF GOD

Having reduced the impact of our angry grief on our emotions, thoughts, relationships, and choices, we are in a better position to consider how pain impacts our view of God. When our emotions are raw, our destructive thoughts sticky, our social sphere restricted, and our choices reactive, it is hard to refine our theology. Decreasing these forms of disruption puts us in a better position to wrestle with the real, difficult questions about God that emerge when we go through painful experiences.

ARTICULATE YOUR QUESTIONS

Asking questions about God when we are angry can feel irreverent. This can cause us to either pull back or surge forward with our questions. Either way, that nagging sense of irreverence lingers. And if we don't feel welcomed to ask our questions—because we feel God disapproves of them or other people do or our own conscience does—it will be hard for us to assimilate any helpful response we get to those questions. In any interaction, when we ask a question, our disposition impacts our ability to process the conversation that follows.

In light of this uneasiness, take a moment to reflect on—even visualize—the implications of Hebrews 4:15–16: "For we do not have a high priest who is unable to sympathize with our weaknesses, but one who in every respect has been tempted [suffered] as we are, yet without sin. Let us then with confidence draw near to the throne of grace, that we may receive mercy and find grace to help in time of need."

Imagine yourself walking up to God to ask a question. Or better, imagine God as a tender father coming to your room knowing you're too upset to talk—that is the implication of the incarnation, that Jesus entered our world. Notice the Greek word for "tempted" can also be translated "suffered." These verses show us that the basis for the confidence with which we pray is God's ability to identify with our hardship.

Consider again the questions you want to ask. Formulate the questions behind your raw emotions from earlier parts of this book. Are they worded in a way that expects a compassionate response? How would you word the questions differently if they were posed to a loving father who came into your room, sat next to you, and asked, "I can tell you're hurt; do you want to talk about it?"

We have done a lot of work on putting your questions into words. Now we want to work on wording our questions in a way that expects them to be received compassionately. We want to do this not because God requires us to "ask nicely," but because it helps us embrace the conversation that follows.

DISTINGUISH REAL FROM TRUE

I remember teaching my youngest son to swim. He was an athletic little kid, but for some reason he was afraid of water. As I picked him up and walked toward the pool, I could tell what he was thinking, *This water is deeper than I am tall. That never goes well for the short guy. You're taking me into the pool. You're not to be trusted.*

He was having a real experience of fear. His heart was thumping so hard I could feel it against my shoulder. His pupils were dilated. His breathing pattern changed. His fear was *real*. But not everything that undergirded his fear was *true*. Nevertheless, this wasn't the time to truth bomb his fear into submission by saying something like, "If I were going to drown you, would I do it in front of this many people?"

To be able to speak to the falseness, or at least incompleteness, of his fear, I needed to affirm the realness of his experience. Knowing I understood him gave him a better basis for trusting what I would say next. That meant saying something similar to, "This feels like a big deal, doesn't it? Learning to swim is a new adventure. It looks like those kids are having fun, doesn't it? I bet you can swim as well as they can. What if we take it slow and learn?"

We can affirm what is real within an emotional experience—in this case, learning to swim is an intimidating challenge—without embracing the untrue content that gets embedded in those emotions—in this case, the pool is perilous and I had ill intent in taking him there.

Now we turn the question to you: "What parts of your emotional experience about God are real but not true?"

You may be surprised to realize that Psalms frequently gives voice to this tension. The psalms express things that are inaccurate about God but that felt true to the author in their moment of distress.

- God is felt to be hiding from us in our troubles (Psalm 10:1)
- God is felt to be forgetful or uninterested in our suffering (Psalm 13:1; 44:24)
- God is felt to have forsaken those who cry out to him (Psalm 22:1–2)
- God is felt to be asleep and therefore unaware (Psalm 44:23)
- God is felt to have abandoned his people forever (Psalm 74:1)
- God is felt to have aggressively "spiked" an innocent person in anger (Psalm 102:10)

What are your versions of these psalms? Distinguishing between what feels real and what is true allows you to begin to doubt these inaccurate statements about God. That is progress. That is what is occurring in these psalms. The author is doubting these statements. We know this because they are addressed as prayers to God. Honest conversational prayers, such as these, are an important part of continuing in the process of grief.

MAKE PEACE WITH THE TENSION

If you read the psalms listed above, you will notice that not all of them end with resolution. Some of them end raw and confused. That is the way relationships are. Undoubtedly, you've experienced conflicts where the issue was resolved—you reached agreement—but your emotions were not resolved. It took time and more interaction for things to feel normal again. But you were willing to spend time and emotional energy for the sake of a valued relationship.

This is where we return to a primary theme of this book; we want to do anger *with* God. That means, for the sake of this valued relationship, we live with the tension for a while. In section 4, we will explore what it looks like to have these more honest conversations with God and to navigate the tensions within our experience to make progress in our grief.

Tension doesn't have to mean we're stuck. Often it means we're growing. Think of the tension that exists as an adolescent becomes a teenager. Too often this phase gets portrayed negatively. But the increased tension means the young person is growing, becoming their own person, and learning what it means to embrace the next season of life. The tension may be uncomfortable, but it's a sign of growth.

When we process painful experiences, our faith becomes less innocent. We are less satisfied with the simple answers that once brought us comfort. Working through angry grief is a lot like being a teenager. We're not leaving the family, but we do want a more robust explanation for what's going on. We may not be fully ready to understand or embrace the explanation we get, but we want to be trusted enough to hear it.

In that sense, our goal in this next phase of our journey is to be a good teenager. We want to ask our honest questions, have the courage to say what doesn't make sense, and engage life in a less innocent way than we have to this point. That's not a bad thing. Much good and much growth can come from it. Less innocent faith can still be strong, God-honoring faith.

QUESTIONS FOR REFLECTION

1. What are the questions about God that your hardship has introduced into your life? How safe or welcomed do you feel to ask these questions?

2. What were some of the important distinctions you made in the real-versus-true section? How does validating your experience of pain or anger help you more objectively evaluate the claims about God that those negative experiences push you toward?

SECTION 4: RESOLVING YOUR GRIEF

Section breaks are a good time to review the big map. We began by establishing a safe context for difficult conversations. Then we put our pain into words. After that, we worked to reduce the various effects of angry grief. Now, we will focus on resolving our grief and gaining the freedom to enjoy the present again.

We will do this work in two ways. First, we will spend two chapters learning to value the gritty faith that emerges after weathering painful experiences. Second, we will spend three chapters reorienting our life toward future goals and dreams rather than past pain.

Chapter 16

VALUING A LESS INNOCENT FAITH

Let's start by defining *innocence*. When we watch children play and think, *They're so innocent*, what are we observing that elicits this reaction? One dimension of their innocence is their innate sense of safety that allows them to play as if everything will be okay, a sense that life is fair and the future will be good.

One reason this innocence stands out to us as adults is that we've lost it. We don't live with an innate sense of safety. We know it takes a lot of hard work and a bit of good fortune for things to turn out okay. We outgrew the idea that life is fair a long time ago. All of this is normal adulthood, adulthood without the painful experiences that would make us angry with God.

This loss of innocence goes by another name: maturity. Maturity is a good thing. While innocence meant we lived fully in the moment without a care in the world, maturity means we anticipate problems, plan for the future, and learn to respond wisely to the unfairness that exists in a broken world. Maturity is resourceful, observant, and anticipatory.

Faith can get disoriented in the transition from innocence to maturity. One reason this transition can be so
hard is that faith is often equated with a naïve innocence
that is blindly optimistic about any hard situation. Conversations with someone who believes a strong faith is an
innocent faith go something like this:

> Alan: "I don't know how I'm going to pay the
> bills after my injury and losing my job."
> Brett: "Don't worry about tomorrow. God has cattle
> on a thousand hills and will take care of everything."

> Alicia: "That person took advantage of me. I don't
> trust them and don't think you should either."
> Beth: "We should believe the best about everyone
> because we're sinners just like they are, and God didn't
> give up on us."

> Aaron: "I don't think my life will ever be the
> same after [traumatic experience]."
> Brandon: "You can trust God has a great plan for
> your life and won't waste any of your suffering."

As we think about rekindling our faith after an experience that caused us to stagnate in angry grief, we fear
conversations with Brett, Beth, or Brandon. Their innocence feels dangerous. Conversations such as these can
create an emotional allergic reaction to the possibility of
embracing hope again. We feel as if hope is a return to
false innocence. But reembracing hope is a core compo-
nent of healthy grieving (1 Thessalonians 4:13).

That brings us to our questions for this chapter: What
does a healthy-but-less-innocent faith look like, and how
do we cultivate it? Stated another way, How do we honor

the maturity that comes amid painful experiences without undermining the hope that is essential for healthy grieving? It is possible. It is not easy. It is worth it.

TALKING WITH NAÏVE FAITH

What is the biggest problem with the responses Brett, Beth, or Brandon are offering? After all, much of what they say could have Bible verses in parentheses after it. When we aren't comforted by what they're saying, then we feel as if we're arguing with God. Their surprised and disapproving look when we don't embrace their optimism only reinforces this notion. When we consider their responses, we can see at least three problems.

1. The *problem of pacing* is how quickly they move toward pronouncing everything okay. If, as you accelerate a car, you skip from first gear to fifth gear, you will blow out the transmission. That is what we do to our souls when we try to (or feel forced to) skip from mourning to rejoicing. The combustion comes out as anger.

2. The *problem of the failure to lament* is their seeming inability to "weep with those who weep" (Romans 12:15). Notice the context for the simple verse, "Jesus wept" (John 11:35). It occurs just moments before Jesus raised his friend Lazarus from the dead. The sinless son of God did not rush his own or anyone else's emotions. We can take from this that God-honoring faith sometimes cries and is willing to be sad.

3. The *problem of perspective* is that they are forcing an end-of-the-journey perspective on a middle-of-the-journey moment. Imagine getting to be a voice-over in the movie trilogy *The Lord of the Rings*. Imagine that in every scene where Frodo is despondent you yelled, "Cheer

up! You win! So, this moment really isn't that bad!" Even though the second statement is true—Frodo wins—that fact doesn't validate the first or third statement. Cheerfulness is not situationally appropriate. The moment is bad and should be honored as such.

When believers assume that in hard times faith should be fast, cheerful, and already containing hindsight, their attempt to encourage faith has mutated into naivety. We don't have to disagree with the biblical truths Brett, Beth, or Brandon cited to be dissatisfied with what they are calling faith. When life is hard, the song of faith will be played in a minor key; that is, robust faith can have notes of weariness and discouragement in it.

LESS INNOCENT FAITH

We can affirm that less innocent faith is not less good or less strong faith. It may be more cautious. However, the degree to which our faith honors God is not diminished simply because it lacks the innocence that was present before our painful experience.

Let's use a biblical parallel. Do you remember the story of the widow's mite (Luke 21:1–4)? Jesus said that the poor widow's gift, although small, was great in value because it was given at greater sacrifice. When faith is expressed out of trust-poverty, a comparable principle is active. God knows and appreciates the sacrifice from which our faith is given. What some might see as a larger expression of innocent faith is not more precious in God's sight than the smaller expression of less innocent faith.

The takeaway from this chapter is that less innocent faith is precious in the eyes of God. It is good, even if the context it emerged from was bad. It will be honored, even though we may fear it will be shamed. The questions are, Do you believe this? Do you value less innocent faith? If not, you may dismiss what God cherishes. You may feel embarrassed about what God admires. If this is you, take a moment to reflect on 1 Corinthians 1:27b-30: "God chose what is weak in the world to shame the strong; God chose what is low and despised in the world, even things that are not, to bring to nothing things that are, so that no human being might boast in the presence of God. And because of him you are in Christ Jesus, who became to us wisdom from God, righteousness and sanctification and redemption."

God has never bought into the economy of achievement, size, and grandeur that we are prone to embrace. We tend to compare ourselves to people around us—and that comparison causes us to fear that our faith is somehow less than their faith. God has never bought into this scoring system. Even before we were hurt, God wanted us to be free from this type of thinking.

We need to learn to see less innocent faith as healthy faith and allow it to nurture healthier emotions. That is where we will turn our attention next. But for now, we can rest in the reality that God will receive our less innocent faith with all the enthusiasm and joy he receives from any other flavor of faith.

QUESTIONS FOR REFLECTION

1. What are the Brett, Beth, or Brandon responses that you fear or brace yourself against?

2. In your own words, how would you name and describe the less innocent faith discussed in this reflection?

Chapter 17

LIVING IN THE TENSION OF PARTIAL UNDERSTANDING

We are continuing to learn about anger so that we can make progress through the angry phase of grief. We are taking the experience of anger in response to pain and turning it like a diamond under a lamp. But, in this case, we are not mesmerized by its beauty; we want to find freedom from its domineering presence in our life.

As we take the next step in our journey, let's consider four facets of anger that revolt against the partial understanding we have of the most painful events in our lives. We will arrange them in a progression to help us grasp the logic of an emotion—anger—that is not always fond of explaining itself.

1. Anger wants certainty.
2. Anger is confident.
3. Anger (artificially) makes fuzzy things clear.
4. Anger interprets the absence of answers as cruel.

Let's unpack this progression.

Anger wants certainty. Anger doesn't want to hear, "Maybe this; maybe that." Anger declares two things: (1) it was wrong, and (2) it mattered. Whoever anger is talking to or about is expected to give a clear explanation of what happened. When someone says, "I don't know," it feels like they're weaseling out by pleading the fifth to avoid saying something incriminating.

As we think about living with a partial understanding of why things happened—as we all do—this desire for certainty adds fuel to the fire of our anger. The lack of a clear explanation exacerbates the anger we feel about our original hurt.

Anger is confident. Anger makes no apologies for its questions. It asks boldly, "Why should we apologize for our questions?" And of course, the answer is we shouldn't. This whole book has been about God welcoming our questions. But sometimes the *way* we ask our questions can be a barrier to progress. We can ask our questions with such force that it makes any reply feel like a debate. If we do this, then it feels as if any helpful response to our pain is God winning and, therefore, us losing.

This is not to say we must speak to God reverently so as not to offend him. We've seen that the psalms are too raw for that logic to stand. The appeal here is simply for us to ask our questions with a dash of humility so that we can have a fruitful conversation about them. It's about our receptivity, not God's fragility.

Anger (artificially) makes fuzzy things clear. Anger wastes no time in connecting dots. If there are two dots on the page—dot 1, I was hurt, and dot 2, God was involved—then anger hastily scribbles a bold line between them: God hurt me. God is not safe. Everything I was told about God was a lie!

At one level, this need for instant clarity is understandable. Confusion and uncertainty add to the painfulness of a situation. It feels like, if we establish meaning—even if it's inaccurate—it will lessen the pain. But that's similar to the student who consoles themselves after failing a test by telling themselves, "The teacher doesn't like me. The test wasn't fair. This class is stupid and is never something I will use in real life." The temporary relief of this meaning-making system comes at the cost of a life marked by blame shifting and excuses.

Anger interprets the absence of answers as cruel. If God won't answer my question, that just proves how little God cares. We can think this pronouncement provides a culmination to our emotional journey. But at best, it enables us to move from being hot-angry with God to cold-aloof. When we're stuck in the anger phase of grief, this feels like the best we can hope for.

This approach assumes there should be a *Karate Kid* moment for all our hardships. We want to know that all the "Paint the fence. Wax the car" training has a "learn some essential skill central to life" outcome. Until we see this positive outcome, we assume God is cruel (see the Additional Resources appendix on page 158 for more on this topic).

What if there was a different and better way to approach our partial understanding?

EMBRACING A PARTIAL UNDERSTANDING

We have just examined the progression of how anger copes with partial understanding. As we try to approach our partial understanding differently, let's look at a new four-part progression. It is not a point–counterpoint to the previous progression. Instead, it is a new approach to the question.

1. We have a partial understanding in an unfolding story.
2. We want to be content with learning, not just knowing.

3. We begin to realize faith is a relationship.
4. We realize our choices impact the outcome.

We have a partial understanding in an unfolding story. The fact that we're grappling with partial understanding means our part in the story is not over. In our pain, we want to stop the story and refuse to continue participating until we get answers to our legitimate questions. Unfortunately, that is not how life works.

Life is not like the repetition of a science experiment. In chemistry class, we could stop at any point to ask the teacher, "Why is it doing that?" And because we were repeating a known experiment, the teacher could answer. Life is not a repeated experiment. Every life is its own journey. The struggles of life may be common to all (1 Corinthians 10:13), but the story of each life is unique.

We want to be content with learning, not just knowing. This is what adds the dash of humility to our angry grief. We don't give up on seeking to understand and create meaning from our hardship; we just realize the process won't be completed as quickly as we prefer.

If we're honest, this realization helps whatever meaning we can make from our pain less insulting. Simple answers aren't adequate for the kind of pain that warrants the journey we're taking together. They come across as trite and cliché. Taking a learning approach rather than an approach that demands quick answers honors the pain we've experienced.

We begin to realize faith is a relationship. We come back to the theme of being angry *with* God. We realize we're not screaming into the night; we're talking to someone who cares. We're not trying to pass a quiz on the historical significance of key events in our life. We are trying to get back to the place where God is a source of rest and refuge, rather than distress and consternation.

Consider having a conversation with God that goes something like this:

> I know you know I'm hurting and confused. You've been patient with me as I've flailed in and railed about my pain. Thank you. But I still don't get it. I still get lost in the pain and confusion. I know you made the ultimate sacrifice at Calvary for my sin. Because of that, I know you have felt the full weight of living in this broken world. I know you cried out, "My God, my God, why have you forsaken me?" (Matt. 27:46). Jesus, you've been on both sides of this conversation. Help me to understand the things I'm able to understand now, to be patient for the things that will be clearer in time, and to lean on you for strength for the things that may never make sense.

This is a relational approach to pain. It is an expression of faith. It doesn't rush us. It accepts the tension of knowing some ultimate things (Jesus's love and compassion toward us) and not knowing some important things (an explanation for our pain). It is better to ask for help in this real tension than to allow our anger to artificially resolve it.

We realize our choices impact the outcome. This final point addresses the feeling of powerlessness that is prevalent in angry grief. When we can't choose what we want most—to erase the painful thing from our life story—we often feel as if we have no choices or ability to meaningfully impact our world. This is not true.

As we have seen, our story is unfolding. A primary factor in how our story unfolds from this point is the choices we make. There are two paths ahead of us.

- *Path 1*: If we remain stagnated in our angry grief, we will make the kind of choices that further the deterioration of our life (see chapter 14). This will add to the cloud of unfairness that hangs over our life and further reinforce the sense of futility that fuels our destructive choices.
- *Path 2*: If we grieve our legitimate pain in a healthier way, it will result in a better life than the first path leads us to. It won't make the sad things untrue. But it can begin to write a future with redemptive and satisfying chapters as an extension of the painful chapters we've been wrestling with.

We may wish we could do a comparative analysis of path 1 and path 2 to get a quantitative assessment of the two resulting lives. But as with any other major life choice, we will never know the other path. We will only know the results of the path we choose. My hope is that our journey together has begun to make path 2 more appealing, not something you feel argued into but something that you genuinely embrace.

QUESTIONS FOR REFLECTION

1. Which of the four facets of how anger sees uncertainty has been the stickiest or most difficult for you?

2. Which of the four realities for embracing a partial understanding of your pain was most meaningful and helpful for you?

Chapter 18

ENGAGING "NEXT"

You may have noticed a general pattern we've cycled through in this book: emotion, cognition, action. We've journeyed this cycle together several times.

Initially, we seek to understand and articulate our emotional experiences. We've treated our emotions as good friends who have something valuable to say.

Then we seek to identify the beliefs expressed by our emotions and the beliefs that would contextualize our emotions in a healthier way. Sometimes we agree with the beliefs that arise from our emotions; other times we sympathetically disagree with them.

Finally, we try to find God-honoring actions that contribute to a flourishing life. Focusing on how our choices impact our lives helps us resist the sense of powerlessness that easily pervades the experience of grief.

In this chapter, we are entering into a new rendition of the action phase. As we do this, it is helpful to start with an observation about grief. We've made many observations about anger, but as we seek to move beyond the anger phase of grief, it will benefit us to get better acquainted with the more vulnerable experience of grief. Our observation for this reflection is this: *when grief stagnates, life stagnates*. We feel stuck. Nothing seems to fit as a good "next" in our life. That stuck feeling is what we want to begin to change.

The key term for this new action phase is *experiment*. We will explore two types of experimentation: cognitive experimentation, or giving yourself the freedom to *consider* new things, and volitional experimentation, or giving yourself the freedom to *try* new things.

Give yourself the freedom to experiment again. When life gets hard, we begin surviving more than living. We don't have the emotional margin to risk trying something that may not work. Living to avoid risk removes the capacity to dream. We want to reinvigorate our capacity to dream.

COGNITIVE EXPERIMENTATION

Your primary goal in cognitive experimentation is to give yourself "first-draft freedom" as you consider new possibilities. When you're writing a first draft, you don't (or, at least, shouldn't) care about the quality of what you're writing. That can be fixed in a second draft. Your initial goal is to get raw material on paper that you can revise later.

As you mentally draft ideas about what might be next for you, allow these seven questions to be brainstorming prompts. Yes, each question has a positive connotation. But this exercise isn't an attempt to make lemonade out of lemons; it's a step toward recultivating a life with positive anticipation.

1. Who are the people you enjoy and want to bless, whether individuals or groups?
2. What roles and activities do you enjoy?
3. What causes are important to you?

4. What truths about life, God, relationships, and so forth, are more real to you now?

5. What talents and aptitudes do you have and enjoy using?

6. What things have felt most normal or good during this difficult season?

7. Imagine yourself ten years from now looking back on the previous decade. What are the key things that would indicate that you have been a good steward of that span of time?

Sit down with some paper or a journal. Write one of these questions at the top of each page and give yourself time to dream. Again, think first draft. Later you can scratch out anything you dislike. You are collecting raw material. Your goal is to begin embracing the idea of a good future again. You want to turn the corner from a life centered on what *was* hard (past tense) to a life focused on what *could be* good (future tense).

This is a common grief transition. In grief prompted by death, we don't always notice it happening. But there comes a point where we quit measuring time with a past-orientation, "It has been # weeks since my loved one died," to a future-orientation, "I've got # days to get ready for [event]." Here, it is not the units of time that are important but our reference for how we're measuring time.

VOLITIONAL EXPERIMENTATION

If the key word for cognitive experimentation was *brainstorm*, the key word for volitional experimentation is *play* or *practice*. It is easy to become inhibited as we move from thoughts to actions because actions feel riskier. Viewing our next steps as play or practice reduces our inhibitions because we know that we aren't looking for an immediate return on our efforts.

Consider the person who is recovering from a significant injury. Their initial efforts at any physical task are going to be less than what they remember being able to do. That doesn't mean they are failing or hopeless. It merely reveals where they are starting the next leg of their journey from.

As you transform your cognitive experimentation list into a plan of action, don't hold yourself to the standard of how easily you did these things before or how much satisfaction you got from comparable activities in the past. Be as kind to yourself as you would be to a friend recovering from a major injury.

With that in mind, start small. Your initial goal is to allow your ability to enjoy people, activities, and roles to thaw. Your first step may be as simple as cooking a meal for a friend and enjoying the conversation that follows. It may be reading the kind of literature you previously enjoyed and taking time to reflect on what was edifying.

As you begin, don't let "all better" get in the way of "a little better." When we're recovering from stagnated grief, we can be our own proverbial child in the back seat of the car asking, "Are we there yet?" When we perpetually monitor our current progress based on where we want to be, we drain the encouragement and enjoyment we could get from seeing the progress we're making.

FROM PLAY TO PURPOSE

As your ability to enjoy a satisfying "next" for your life thaws, begin to think about the larger purpose(s) you want to live for again. Allow the smaller enjoyments to create momentum to jump-start your larger dreams. This is where you begin to ask, What does it look like to steward the next season of my life for the glory of God?

If you have been processing this book *with* God—an approach we have tried to cultivate—then the idea of living for the glory of God is less distressing than when we began. You have experienced God's kindness and patience in such way that sharing that compassion with others is an appealing possibility (2 Corinthians 1:3–5).

If experimenting with the larger purpose you want to live for is overwhelming, don't feel rushed. Just know that possibility is there. The Christian life is not a competition. God is not comparing us to one another. God delights in seeing each of his children take the next step in their journey. Continue at your pace and trust in God's care.

QUESTIONS FOR REFLECTION

1. Where or how have you noticed the stagnation of grief in your life?

2. What steps in your cognitive or volitional experimentation are you considering?

Chapter 19

BUT I'M RIGHT!?!

As you consider engaging the future with purpose and hope, there is a common refrain that is likely to echo in your mind: "But I'm right! I wasn't wrong about what happened." The really bad things did happen. They weren't primarily your fault. And yet, you are the one stuck in your grief. As optimism begins to gain momentum, you may need to grapple again with this common obstacle to grieving well.

When grief is prompted by death, we don't have to worry about being wrong. No one is trying to convince us to see things differently. In a sense, that allows us to grieve with confidence and freedom.

But in grief prompted by painful life events, we might be right. Often, we are. The betrayal was wrong and wasn't "just an accident." The negligence was real, and we are the one paying the highest price—even though we had nothing to do with it. We weren't excessive in our expectation but were still disappointed. The disease was random and there wasn't anything we could have done to prevent it.

Nevertheless, Christian friends often try to either persuade us that we might be wrong or ask us to be humble enough to not ask hard questions. They may insinuate that we're wrong by bringing up the truth that none of us is ultimately innocent. Saying this suggests that we must be utterly innocent (i.e., completely without sin) to ask honest questions about hardships we're facing.

If our choices caused our pain, the life assessments we've done to this point would have revealed that. When we're wrong, it is good and right to realize and acknowledge it. But for this discussion, we are going to assume you are right; that is, your actions did not cause the hardship you're facing.

But being right about our pain doesn't circumvent the need for grief. And we don't have to be perfect for God to have compassion toward our suffering. So, we ask the question, How do we grieve when we're right about our hardship and innocent of causing it?

Before I offer guidance on this question, there is one more acknowledgment that needs to be made: *grieving when we're right about painful events may be the most difficult form of grief.* As we seek to gain a sense of direction in our grief, we will try to understand grief-when-we're-right by walking through four realities that help us make sense of the confusion.

1. Grief doesn't mean admitting you were wrong; it means allowing the season in which your life was defined by your pain to conclude.
2. Grief, whether caused by death or another painful event, means that you live in a broken world.
3. Grief demands hope that is larger than this temporal world.
4. Grief means you embrace the future with hope.

Grief doesn't mean admitting you were wrong; it means allowing the season in which your life was defined by your pain to conclude. Progress in grief means your current season of life is no longer defined by the pain from the previous season of life. You can be right about the pain and still make this transition. With a bit of reflection, you should be able to see that this transition is healthy and good.

As we have seen, life lived in reaction to pain takes on an unhealthy pattern. Actions that are reactive, that are driven by the desire to escape our pain, can bring us harm. To visualize this principle, imagine your pain is a bear. It is easy to think that anywhere "away" from the bear is a good direction to run. But "away" from the bear may take you "toward" a cliff or "into" a bear trap. Grieving your pain is what allows you to quit living in reaction to the bear and begin to choose the direction you want life to move "toward." You can be right about the past and still choose the direction in life you want to pursue next.

Grief, whether caused by death or another painful event, means that you live in a broken world. Realizing that we live in a broken world helps us end our mental rehearsals. In an unbroken world, we would be able to get to a place where the things that happened made sense and everyone agreed about them.

Think of an unbroken world as the teacher's grading sheet for a math test. We assume all the answers are correct. If we're confused about how to do the problem, we work backward from the answer to the initial equation to try to figure out what needs to be done. In an unbroken world, we spend our energy figuring out how the confusing things make sense—and we find that they do.

Now, think of our broken world as the student's test that is being graded. If there is a wrong answer, we might try to understand the student's logic to help them work the equation correctly. But we accept that there will be errors in the student's logic, not just in their final answer. In grief, acknowledging we live in a broken world, with broken people, as a broken person helps us let go of the notion that everything should make sense.

Grief demands hope that is larger than this temporal world. But realizing we live in a broken world, by itself, is not as satisfying as we need it to be. We want to know that a right answer to the equation exists (continuing the math metaphor) and that eventually people will agree on it. This is especially true because what prompted our pain was not mathematics but injustice.

We don't mind striving if there is some hope for resting. But perpetual striving is exhausting, physically and emotionally. Accepting that the world will always be broken—with no hope for ultimate justice or restoration—would be like that. It is unsatisfying for a parent who lost a child to an accident caused by a drunk driver to hear, "People aren't perfect. Humans are prone to addiction. That's just part of human nature."

If our grief is going to become unstuck, we want to know that there is more of an answer than this, even if this is all the answer we have access to right now. That is what it means to grieve with hope (1 Thessalonians 4:13). We may not grieve as those who have acquired what we want—namely, a world where our pain would never occur—but, because of the gospel, we can grieve as those who have hope.

This doesn't mean that the hope of heaven erases the significance of our pain. That would be insulting; similar to telling a child, "Don't cry because your dog died, because you're going to have a great birthday party next month." It does mean our pain doesn't get the final word. Evil doesn't win. Chaos won't reign.

Progress in grief means we can endure what is still hard because we know we will not have to endure forever. This is why the picture of heaven as a place of rest is precious (Hebrews 4:3–4). The hard work of grieving will eventually end.

Grief means you embrace the future with hope. This is where we will turn our attention next. We will seek to answer the question, How can I trust hope again? Our progression in thought to this point has helped us see the role of hope in grief and to see how progress in grief provides the freedom from anger we've been seeking. We have seen that the gospel is the source of the hope that makes this progress possible.

Even still, you may be saying, "I know, but…" This "but" doesn't have to mean that you disbelieve the gospel; too often our continued emotional disturbance is interpreted this way. The "but" often means, "I can intellectually assent that these things are true. I believe them. But they don't settle my emotions like it seems they should. I struggle to trust the hope I believe."

That is what we will consider in the next chapter.

QUESTIONS FOR REFLECTION

1. How do you describe the difference between grief prompted by death and grief prompted by other painful life events?

2. Where in the progression of this chapter's four realities do you tend to get stuck?

Chapter 20

TRUSTING HOPE AGAIN

As we've journeyed out of the anger phase of grief, we have learned a great deal about ourselves and how we experience emotions. Growth does that. Growth results in our getting to know ourselves more clearly and accurately. We increase our ability to name and understand our experience, so we can bring those experiences to God more openly. The same kind of growth will take place as we explore trusting hope again.

When we've been through something painful enough to create a rupture in our relationship with God, it is not just our relationship with God that is damaged. Negative experiences of this magnitude cause us to mistrust hope as much as we mistrusted God. Those are not the same thing. It's worth understanding why.

Mistrust toward God is mistrust toward the character of a person. Mistrusting hope is a more generalized fear of being disappointed again. When we mistrust hope, it is hard to trust God or anyone else. We begin to treat any positive expectation as if it is threat. Part of restoring our relationship with God is getting to the point where we no longer view hope and gullibility as synonyms.

We have all had times when we have mistrusted hope. We have disappointed ourselves, experienced pain because of it, grown pessimistic, and as a result, become skeptical toward the notion that things could ever be better again.

Maybe you failed a test, studied hard for the next one, and yet, despite being adequately prepared, had a difficult time believing you would do well. Perhaps you hit a slump in your sport of choice, practiced hard, improved your skills, yet still went into the next game pessimistic. Or, maybe you were hurt in a relationship, identified the red flags you missed, but still struggled to trust the next nice person who didn't have those red-flag qualities.

These are examples of struggling to trust hope—to believe that the future can be good again—after a painful experience. It is not that you mistrusted a person: the teacher who said you were ready for the test, the coach who commented on your improvement, or your friends who affirmed the character of the potential new dating partner. You mistrusted hope itself. But this mistrust of hope impaired the relationships with your teacher, coach, and friends. That is the dynamic we are trying to navigate in your relationship with God.

If we had to pick a word that accounted for this allergic reaction to hope, it would be risk. We want to be certain that things will be different next time. We don't want there to be any room for error. Our standard for the probability of success is so high that it suffocates our emotions and paralyzes our choices. Hope involves accepting some degree of risk, and so we avoid it.

This avoidance of risk characterized the angry phase of our grief. Anger made us feel impenetrable; we cut ourselves off from anything or anyone that required us to trust. This made us feel safe but at the cost of being lonely. Our suspicion of hope became a significant part of the wedge between us and God, even as God wanted to comfort us amid our suffering.

Grief has been healthily processed when we can open ourselves to hope and have a realistic optimism about the future again. This realistic optimism, however, requires that we become less suspicious and more willing to trust. To restore our ability to trust hope, we will consider a five-step process that summarizes and extends the journey we've been on.

5 STEPS TOWARD TRUSTING HOPE

Step 1: Trust begins with honesty. Our entire journey has been about being more honest with God, self, and others. In many ways, honesty is the currency of trust. This is more than a poetic metaphor. It can give us insight into how trust works in our life.

Let's consider the metaphor of currency. Sometimes we spend money wisely, and it feels good (perhaps buying a loved one a present). Sometimes we spend money wisely, and it feels unpleasant (maybe paying off a debt or buying something mundane like insurance). But the more we dispense our finances wisely, the more our overall sense of life satisfaction increases. It is true that money can't buy happiness, but money spent poorly can accrue massive quantities of misery.

The same is true with the currency of honesty for trust. Sometimes trust feels good (like being truly known by a friend); other times it may make us feel uneasy (like the apprehension just after we've been vulnerable). But the more we wisely dispense trust, the more life satisfaction we experience. This is not an absolute, watertight rule, but similar to the principles we find in Proverbs, it is a wise and generally reliable life principle.

Be as honest about your response to the idea of trusting hope as you've been about everything else in this book. Even if that honesty means expressing apprehension. Being honest about your angst—with God, self, and good friends—is the initial step in cultivating a healthier relationship with trust.

Step 2: Identify the risk. When we struggle with trust, the natural question to ask is, What's at stake? The simple, honest answer is usually, "I don't want to be hurt like that again." But our mistrust of hope means that our fear has generalized beyond just an aversion to being hurt like that to a fear of being hurt at all.

To examine your struggle to trust hope, reflect on these questions. Again, some questions will fit your situation more than others. Feel free to just focus on the ones that provide fruitful considerations.

- What does your mistrust of hope fear losing? What does it keep from happening?
- To what other people or situations has your mistrust of hope generalized?
- If your mistrust of hope could talk, what would it say?
- If you could change one thing to alleviate your mistrust of hope, what would it be? Why?
- What is your mistrust of hope costing you? What makes the sacrifice seem worthwhile to you?

Your goal in this step is to be able to complete this sentence: If I grow in my trust of hope, it will mean being willing to risk [blank]. In answering this question, you are changing your perspective on what progress means from feeling pleasant in previously uncomfortable situations to naming the specific sacrifice you're willing to consider. Perhaps your "blank" is being misunderstood, as you were in the hurtful situation. In that case, progress means being able to identify when a new friend merits trust and being willing to make the sacrifice of vulnerability when they do.

Step 3: Don't overreact by calling folly "faith." Sometimes when we get clarity (i.e., an answer to the question above), we become too bold. We try to learn to swim in the pool of faith by jumping into the proverbial deep end. We consider it a spiritual version of ripping off the Band-Aid.

If we do this, our good intentions can result in folly. Maybe you tell yourself in advance that you are going to pursue the next dating opportunity that arises or say yes to the next ministry opportunity that presents itself. Such resolutions may address the risk you need to be willing to take, but they also are a form of "throwing caution to the wind."

A better approach is to share what you need to be more willing to risk with one or two trusted friends. Commit to being honest with them when an opportunity arises to take this kind of risk. Invite them to help you assess the opportunity. This approach will help you not be emotionally reactive as you begin to allow your trust in hope to thaw.

Step 4: Realize that faith itself is a risk. Risk is inherent in faith. Where certainty exists, faith is unnecessary. Similarly, sacrifice is inherent in worship. Worship that doesn't cost us anything is just celebration. We see this principle in Romans 12:1, "I appeal to you therefore, brothers, by the mercies of God, to present your bodies as a *living sacrifice*, holy and acceptable to God, which is *your spiritual worship*" (emphasis added).

This is true in any relationship. When we are in love, we sacrifice time to be with the person we love. When we love our job or a hobby, we sacrifice other interests to become better at it. Love, which is worship, expresses itself in sacrifice.

In good times, these sacrifices don't feel like sacrifices at all. It is simply what we most want to do. We often think that worship should only feel like this kind of delight. But, in hard times, sacrifices do feel like sacrifices. But we still say that they're worth it. It is this "worth-it-ness" that makes these sacrifices acts of worship.

Here are several points to help you implement steps 3 and 4 in this process.

- Articulate the precious things you are cautious about sacrificing. Your journey to this point should give you a deep appreciation for why and how these things became precious.
- Vet the decisions related to these sacrifices with trusted friends to make sure they are wise.
- If it is wise, make the sacrifice of trust by following through on your decisions as an expression that God is worth it.
- If it is not wise, allow this process to build your trust as you realize God does not ask you to be reckless as a sign of blind devotion.

Step 5: Make the sacrifice without trying to "have your cake and eat it too." This is where we often get stuck because we want to think that, with God, we shouldn't really have to make sacrifices. We think that faith in God is similar to a college graduate paying rent to their parents to live at home for a year after college and the parents save that money for the child to use as the down payment on their first house. Yes, it's a sacrifice but not really.

Sometimes this rent-becomes-down-payment scenario does happen. We sacrifice, and God blesses us in ways that more than offset the sacrifice we made. It is wonderful when this happens. But if that is what we expect to happen, we become transactional in our relationship with God. Then if our expectations aren't met, we begin to think God failed us, let us down, or broke his promises.

Consider Paul's sacrifices of trust as he planted churches. Paul's sacrifices resulted in significant hardships: illness, shipwreck, broken relationships, and jail (2 Corinthians 11:16–33). At many points on these journeys, we might say that Paul's return on these sacrifices wasn't greater than the hardship he faced. Paul was honest about this. He acknowledged that his anguish was sometimes as dark as we could imagine, to the point of despairing of life itself. Yet, Paul also wanted people to know that these sacrifices were "worth it."

Second Corinthians 1:8–11 is an example of the kind of honesty and testimony you have been cultivating on this journey.

> For we do not want you to be unaware, brothers, of the affliction we experienced in Asia. For we were so utterly burdened beyond our strength that we despaired of life itself. Indeed, we felt that we had received the sentence of death. But that was to make us rely not on ourselves but on God who raises the dead. He delivered us from such a deadly peril, and he will deliver us. On him we have set our hope that he will deliver us

again. You also must help us by prayer, so that many will give thanks on our behalf for the blessing granted us through the prayers of many.

Take heart in the reality that God inspired one of the most passionate Christians of all time to record his testimony about struggling to trust hope, to believe that his sacrifices were "worth it." God knew we need testimonies like this so that we don't think he is absent or ambivalent toward our seasons of struggling, which will help us trust hope again.

QUESTIONS FOR REFLECTION

1. What are examples of how you have seen a mistrust of hope become generalized in your life?

2. Which step in the five steps toward trusting hope best captures what you are working on right now?

SECTION 5: CONTEXTUALIZING YOUR JOURNEY IN THE GOSPEL

To this point our focus has been on journey and process more than theology. Yes, we have frequently referenced important theological themes, but your experience has been at the forefront of our work. In section 5, we want to balance out this emphasis.

This final section will not introduce much new material. Rather, it will reorganize the content we've discussed, so that it aligns with the five major movements of the gospel: creation, fall, redemption, sanctification, and glorification. The goal for this section is to help you map the personal progress you've made onto the big themes of the gospel.

Chapter 21

CREATION
WHY WE EXPECT GOOD THINGS

We are turning a corner as we begin this final section. While our entire journey has been biblically based and theologically informed, in this last leg of our journey, we will seek to assimilate the progress made into the major themes of the gospel.

OUR FIRST QUESTION

We could have started this book by asking, Why are we surprised and upset when bad things happen? If we live in a survival-of-the-fittest world, where everything is random, why do we have the expectation that good things should occur? Because our goals were to process pain and grieve healthily we did not start with this question. However, at this point in our journey, the question merits our attention.

Often, we miss the extent to which our belief that the world should be just is based on the assumption that it was created by a loving and fair God (Genesis 1:31). The belief that life randomly progressed from micro-organisms to intelligent, moral beings and that eventually another life form will supplant humans as the most advanced creatures on this planet doesn't give us a reason to expect life to be fair.

In a way, our anger was right to assume God was the problem. At least, God is the reason we feel such inner turmoil when injustice occurs; without God, we would expect life to be a free-for-all where only the strongest survive and, therefore, might makes right. But because God made this world to be good and we are made in his image, we get emotionally disrupted when things go painfully awry.

WE'RE NOT CRAZY

This means as we take this journey of grieving our pain, we're not crazy. We are not trying to decode a message in the white noise of a television set without an antenna. We are looking at the shattered pieces of a beautiful work of art, saddened that it's broken, and wondering how to put it back together again.

The creation phase in the Bible was short-lived, only two chapters (Genesis 1–2). Although brief, it lays a foundation that is vital for our emotional regulation. It tells us that we are not naïve, immature children when we respond as if the world was meant to be a good place.

Genesis 1 and 2 affirm your pain. Creation means that God, the Creator, was the first to feel pain at the world's being broken, and the pain we feel is an echo of his pain. What God feels is deeper than a mere sympathetic response to our hardships. Imagine what it was like for the heart of God when the initial sin shattered his masterpiece of creation. What we imagine, God remembers.

God has never forgotten what he intended this world to be. That is why, at the end of time, he will establish a new heaven and new earth (Revelation 21). God is committed to seeing his original intent fulfilled and enjoyed. But, in the meantime, God is redeeming what was broken. We will talk about this process in the gospel themes to come, but from the creation theme, you should receive an affirmation. God agrees with you; more accurately, your grief affirms God's response to the marring of goodness because he felt it first.

ANOTHER METAPHOR

Imagine the goodness of creation like a beautiful melody, a song. Now imagine that this song of songs is being played by a middle school band. You can still distinguish the original melody, but you can also tell it's not the same.

This picture captures much of what our current experience of the goodness of creation is like. There is enough of God's fingerprint remaining on the sin-scarred world that we still see it, hear it, feel it, and long for it. And when God's creation goodness is disrupted, we get upset—sometimes sad, other times angry. But hearing the melody of God's creation goodness reminds us not to give in to the cloud of cynicism that so easily settles over our lives in this broken world.

So, as you reflect on this first theme of the gospel, the implication is simply: do not relinquish your expectation and aspiration that things be good. Both your anger and your grief have been evidences that you haven't. It is callousness and cynicism that evidence a surrender of the idea that things should be good and can be again. The goodness of creation reminds us that it is better to feel than not to feel—even if the emotions are unpleasant—when we see God's good design being marred.

QUESTIONS FOR REFLECTION

1. What is your response to the idea that your anger and your grief have been an affirmation that God created this world to be good?

2. What is your response to the idea that your grief echoes God's own grief at the marring of his good creation?

Chapter 22

FALL
WHY GOOD EXPECTATIONS HURT

Maybe you've read or watched The Lord of the Rings (LOTR) trilogy. Fans of LOTR will say that you must understand *The Hobbit* to understand LOTR. *The Hobbit* is where you meet Bilbo, encounter the ring with its strange powers, and get to know the geography and inhabitants of Middle Earth. The drama of LOTR only makes sense in light of *The Hobbit*. In this chapter, we will see that Genesis 3 is the equivalent of *The Hobbit* for the rest of the Bible.

Genesis 3 is the account of the fall, the moment when sin entered and marred creation through the choices of Adam and Eve. Everything else in the Bible is about correcting the damage that permeated creation in Genesis 3. According to the Bible, everything that goes wrong in our lives—the bad things we do (sin) and the hard things that happen to us (suffering)—have their origin in Genesis 3.

We ended the creation reflection by noting how the goodness of creation affirms the pain we feel. Unfortunately, affirmation does not remove hurt. We may feel understood, and that is better than the alternative. But having a theological explanation for our pain doesn't anesthetize it, just as understanding the cause and effects of a concussion doesn't alleviate the headaches and nausea.

So, you may ask, why are we considering the fall? If it won't make our pain go away, what good will it do? Those are fair questions. While there is momentary relief in realizing we're not going to try to explain your pain away, this relief is quickly followed by the question, Well, what are we going to do?

REMOVING THE SHOCK FACTOR

We're considering the fall to remove some (not all) of the shock from our pain. But we tread lightly here because it's not the personal shock we are removing. We may still ask, How could *you* [i.e., spouse, pastor, friend, teacher] do *that* [i.e., betrayal or offense] to me? The bonds of trust that allowed us to be hurt mean it was appropriate for us to be surprised. Not being surprised means we live with a deep level of cynicism, one that impairs our emotions and relationships in noncrisis times.

But an accurate understanding of the fall does remove some of the shock that it could happen at all. For some of us, it is easy to succumb to the mistaken notion that we live in a good world with good people. When we believe we live in a good world, profoundly painful experiences make it feel as if a supervillain invaded a romantic comedy.

By way of illustration, if I'm at a haunted house and someone jumps out from behind a door with a knife, I scream like a little girl, catch my breath, and scowl at the feigned attacker. I didn't fully know what to expect, but I was expecting something bad. However, if the same thing happens at my home, I fight for my life. An awareness of the fall means we realize we live in a world haunted by the effects of sin.

Actually, it gets worse. The fall means we are all capable of more evil than we care to imagine. The fall reminds us that, apart from the grace of God, we are all capable of the kinds of betrayals and offenses that have disrupted our lives. The depth of the problem of sin is why Jesus had to come and die to pay the "wages" (Romans 6:23) of sin on our behalf. The pain that prompted our angry grief should give us a deeper appreciation for the weight of why Jesus came and the significance of what Jesus did.

A word of caution might be needed here. Too often Christians misuse the truth that we are all sinful. It becomes a "the ground is level at the foot of the cross" appeal that reminds us that we are just as guilty before God as the person(s) who hurt us. That is true, but it is not the point being made here. Further, making this point to someone who is processing a betrayal poorly represents God's redemptive agenda.

When someone is rescued from a burning building, God's response isn't to remind them, "You know, hell is a lot hotter than that fire, and without Jesus you will feel that for eternity." God doesn't use moments of suffering to send sin-zingers. After bringing us out of the burning building, God will comfort us for the fear and grief that result from living in a broken world where homes burn. That is the point we are making.

If you read Romans 8:19–24, this is the pastoral appeal Paul is making when he notes that all of creation groans under the weight of the fall. In its own way, each part of creation feels the effects of the fall and cries out in agony. Every part of creation harmonizes with our yearning for the curse of sin to be lifted. You live in a world where every plant, rock, and animal you see shouts an "Amen!" to your exasperation.

It is in this context that we are less surprised that pain and betrayal happen, though we can still be surprised by the specific circumstances in which they occur.

In that sense, living in a fallen world is like having a teenage driver in your home. You know you are likely to get a phone call that he or she has gotten in a wreck. On the day that the call comes, you are surprised-but-not-surprised. You didn't wake up and think, *Today is the day*. You had other plans for what needed to get done. And your growing trust in their developing skill behind the wheel only adds to your surprised-but-not-surprised feeling. Pain in a post-Genesis-3 reality is a lot like that.

AVOIDING CYNICISM

So, what do we do with this reminder of where we are in the story of redemption? Understanding where we are in the redemptive journey helps us avoid succumbing to cynicism (see the Additional Resources appendix on page 158 for more on this topic). Cynicism is the disposition that believes it can see through any good situation or action to the bad situation or motive that underlies it. The problem with cynicism is that it believes it can see through everything. All of life becomes a window— something transparent we see through—and nothing is a tree—something solid and real.

If the story of redemption stopped at the fall, cynicism would be the most rational response. Hope would be a form of denial. But because the gospel story continues, we can be hopeful realists. We can acknowledge that bad things are bad—even that evil things are truly evil. The fall explains why there is no need for minimization. But the rest of the gospel story, as we will see, says that we can be honest about the world in which we live and still have hope because evil does not get the final word.

QUESTIONS FOR REFLECTION

1. How has your sense of shock about what happened to you changed during your journey to resolve your grief? How does understanding the implications of the fall help remove some of that shock?

2. When has the cynical struggle of seeing through everything good been most difficult for you? How has that changed during this journey?

Chapter 23

REDEMPTION
AN ANSWER . . . SORT OF

The title of this chapter probably will get two, strongly conflicting responses. Some people will fear it verges on heresy to imply the gospel is only "sort of" the answer. Other people will be relieved at the recognition that embracing the Christian belief system doesn't immediately take us into "happily ever after." The title is meant to draw out this tension, so we can speak to it directly. Both sides make valid points.

To help us navigate this tension, imagine a movie where the plotline involves a virus afflicting the entire world. In this movie the casualty rate is high, families lose loved ones, economies are ravaged, dreams for the future are made unobtainable, and fear dominates. Then an antidote is found. Through the miracle of cinematic time lines, this antidote is produced and delivered on a scale that puts an end to the virus worldwide. Hope now invades the story.

This is where most movies quickly end. If we follow a typical movie plotline, it has several key stages. There is an introduction where we get to know the main characters. Then the angst is introduced when a problem arises. The main part of the movie is the buildup to resolving the angst. Next is the climax, the emotional high point of the movie. Finally, there is the conclusion where loose ends are tied up. This is usually the briefest part of the movie, less than ten minutes in a two-hour film.

As you can probably tell, I'm building an analogy. The virus in our movie represents sin and the effects of the fall. The antidote represents the gospel as God's remedy and our ultimate source of hope. The gospel invades our life with hope. But this is where the metaphor breaks down. The post-climactic part of our lives is not the briefest part of our lives. By contrast, it is often the longest.

Let's continue our movie analogy. What would be different if the movie were built on a real-life time line rather than a cinematic time line? We would follow the main characters' lives as the hope the antidote brought began to give way to the weight of grief over lost family members, uncertainty over future ambitions, and the hardships of living in a broken economy. The hope would be real, but it would be muddled with many other equally real concerns.

How does this help us understand redemption? Even if the main problem has been solved (i.e., the gospel paying our sin debt), the aftershocks of that problem still create significant life disruption (i.e., the effects of sin and the fall). The gospel is the remedy for the virus of sin that has infected us all. Yes, and amen! This is the only hope for the human race. But the ramifications of the fall persist and must be endured. Celebrating one does not require minimizing the other.

FOUR IMPLICATIONS

Let's consider four implications of this tension between the ultimate hope of the gospel and the ongoing effects of the fall.

First, the gospel means that we face real hardships with real hope. Place yourself back in our fictitious movie. When the virus had no cure, what did you want more than anything else? Answer: hope. When there was no cure, planting a garden seemed futile. What's the point if we're not going to be alive to eat the vegetables?

After the virus had a cure, hard things still needed to be done, and harsh realities still had to be faced. But these hardships could be faced knowing the effort being put forward was not futile. Ultimate hope for survival gave significance to everything that needed to be done. It did not make that work easy, but it made it meaningful.

Second, the gospel rewrites the future rather than rewriting the past. We wish the gospel rewrote our life script in both directions. It does not. The difficult things are real. If those hard things are our sin, they have been forgiven and their power to interfere with our relationship with God has been eliminated. If those hard things are suffering, then we have the comfort of knowing they will not have the last word over our lives.

Whether we have been affected by sin or suffering, the gospel means that the effects of the fall will come to an end when we see Jesus face-to-face. The gospel means that we can experience more and more of the freedom this reality brings between now and then (more on that in the next chapter).

In other words, the gospel means that our forever future will be free from the effects of the fall and that our temporal future can be incrementally freer from the effects of the fall. Our work in this book has been about experiencing more of this temporal freedom through the gospel. But whatever freedom we experience will come from redemptively incorporating the hard things into our life story, not seeing them erased.

Third, ultimate hope still requires temporal struggle. Being freer from the effects of the fall is not the same as being free. We still live in a broken world as fallen people in relationship with other fallen people. To use the example God first used in Genesis 3 to describe it, we still live in a world with weeds.

The same frustration we experience within ourselves after salvation—the frustration that selfishness, pride, cowardice, and other sins did not vanish—is being experienced by everyone around us. We do have ultimate hope, but the experience of this hope is not as complete and instantaneous as we prefer.

We live in the tension of celebrating this ultimate hope and grieving the things are not "on earth as [they are] in heaven" (Matthew 6:10). That we are encouraged to pray this prayer and that we *need* to pray it reveals the tension in which we live. Jesus invites us to pray this way as a promise the prayer will be answered, but the necessity to pray for these things reveals the continued weediness of our lives.

Fourth, following profoundly hard experiences, we may still have scars even after we embrace the gospel. In John 20:24–29, we notice that Jesus's perfect, post-resurrection body still has scars. Jesus's scars give us a fitting picture of our already-not-yet life between embracing the gospel and arriving in heaven. For now, at least, we have hope with scars.

This is part of the less innocent, still good faith we discussed in chapter 16. Like physical scars, when treated well, our emotional scars shrink, and the pain beneath them dissipates. Healing our scars has been a focus of our journey. But although we dream of our emotional scars being completely gone and the memory of them erased, that is more than we are promised this side of heaven.

In the next chapter, we will consider the fourth major theme of the gospel: sanctification. This is where we will consider how to squeeze as much temporal healing as possible from the ultimate hope of the gospel for the hardships we have faced.

We'll turn our attention to sanctification with the anticipation that emerges from that hope. When our grief was stunted in the anger phase, one of the things we lost was anticipation—the longing for a positive future. Understanding the power of the gospel revives anticipation so that we look to the work of sanctification with positive expectation.

QUESTIONS FOR REFLECTION

1. How did the analogy of the movie about the virus and its cure help you understand the hope of the gospel and how we experience it?

2. Which of the four implications of the gospel is the most meaningful for where you are on your journey?

Chapter 24

SANCTIFICATION
A MESSY JOURNEY
IN A BROKEN WORLD

Sanctification may come across as a fancy theological word. Don't be intimidated. Simply put, sanctification is the process of becoming more like Jesus. When we embrace the gospel, God erases our sin debt, and we gain the assurance of eternity with God in heaven. That is justification. It occurs in a moment. For the rest of our earthly life, we experience progressive sanctification. It happens with ebbs and flows and in new ways during each season of life.

As we think about sanctification in light of the journey we've been taking together, one of the challenges for us is that we usually only think of sanctification in terms of purification from sin. Removing sin from our lives is a vital part of sanctification. We do want to see the desires of our heart that make sin enticing shrink. The metaphor of pruning is often used for this aspect of sanctification (John 15:1–5); our sinful tendencies are cut away so that we will experience greater growth and bear more good fruit in our lives. This pruning can be painful—but even when it is, it is good, and we should thank God for it.

But if we only think of sanctification in terms of purification, we begin to believe that every unpleasant emotion that emerges from suffering reveals an idol, some aspect of life taking on a God-sized role in our heart. This belief is inaccurate, creates false guilt, and causes God to come across as an uncaring cosmic Cop. An incomplete view of sanctification makes it difficult to process grief that has stagnated in the anger phase.

So, we ask, What is the complementary aspect of sanctification that needs to be emphasized? If sanctification is the process of becoming more Christlike, the following question will point us to the answer. What verb does the Bible use to describe Jesus's response to suffering? Consider what Hebrews 12:2 says of Jesus: "Looking to Jesus, the founder and perfecter of our faith, who for the joy that was set before him *endured* the cross, despising the shame, and is seated at the right hand of the throne of God" (emphasis added).

We become like Jesus when we endure suffering in a way that resists the shame that often accompanies it. We need a view of sanctification that allows us to both be purified from sin without a condemning sense of guilt and endure suffering without a stigmatizing sense of shame. That is what it is to be Christlike in a broken world where sin and suffering are both common experiences.

We will consider both *sanctification via purification* and *sanctification via endurance* to further consolidate the progress you've made on this journey. Hopefully, realizing that sanctification is not just about purification will provide the emotional freedom to grow in the areas where some desires have grown too large, which is inevitably true of all of us.

SANCTIFICATION VIA PURIFICATION

This is where we ask the question, What has become so important to me that I have been willing to sin in response to my pain? Perhaps your drive for achievement made the setbacks resulting from your hardship unbearable, so you cheated to catch up. Maybe your heightened desire for loyalty led you to view any correction as betrayal, so you judge faithful feedback from friends as a personal attack.

Notice something about both examples. Achievement and loyalty are good things. We should not feel bad for wanting them. They are good expectations of healthy people and healthy relationships. As we do the soul-searching work of sanctification, we are merely asking if they became too important. Like a swollen ankle, we want to shrink their importance, not amputate them.

This brings us to another often-neglected aspect of sanctification. When engaged well, sanctification should focus on motives as much as actions. Yes, we want to commit fewer sinful actions, such as cheating and judging in the examples above. But we also want our sinful motives—the desires that make sin enticing—to decrease. Unless both forms of change are occurring, our underlying character is not really becoming more like Christ.

Why bring this up? It is important to realize that sanctification via purification brings freedom. In the examples above, if achievement and loyalty were less important (not unimportant), the urge to cheat or judge would dissipate. This is a good thing—something we should want to happen, and something a loving God wants for us. When we realize this, we see that sanctification via purification is a gift, not a punishment.

SANCTIFICATION VIA ENDURANCE

This is where we ask the question, What parts of life have become more meaningful as a result of what I have experienced? In Hebrews 12:2, we see that Jesus allowed the meaningfulness of what his death would accomplish—namely, salvation for those who accept his sacrifice on their behalf—to enable him to endure the cross.

Take a moment and reflect on the people you know who have suffered well. What is true about them? We usually greatly admire their perspective on life. They have an ability to maintain focus on the things that really matter. They can persevere through discouragement for things that they deem "worth it." We admire the wisdom and resilience their suffering produced.

This is the kind of growth we are seeking to glean from sanctification via endurance. It's what Paul described in Romans 5:3–5: "Not only that, but we rejoice in our sufferings, knowing that suffering produces endurance, and endurance produces character, and character produces hope, and hope does not put us to shame, because God's love has been poured into our hearts through the Holy Spirit who has been given to us."

We often become distracted by the verb *rejoice* in verse 3. Paul is not celebrating the experience of suffering; he is affirming the outcomes of suffering well: endurance, character, hope, freedom from shame, and a realization of God's continued love. That is what we want to do as we consolidate the progress we've made on this journey. We want to affirm the ways we've grown through endurance.

Ask yourself the following questions:

- How has my suffering cemented the importance of primary things I used to take for granted?
- What secondary or tertiary things are proportionally less important to me than they were before?
- How has my ability to resist distraction by secondary or tertiary things increased?
- How has my willingness to persevere for primary things increased?

As you answer these questions, try to frame your responses in a way that does not center on your pain. For instance, instead of saying, "I don't care about what negative people think of me anymore," you might say, "I've realized who the people are I want to speak into the significant decisions of my life. That simplifies decisions and stabilizes my emotions. I enjoy life more and make better decisions because of it."

This change isn't about superficially being more positive. It is about experiencing more freedom. As we grieve in a healthy way, we will decentralize the hard things as we think about day-to-day life. Notice, from Hebrews 12, this is what Jesus did. Jesus did not focus on those who would not accept his sacrifice on their behalf (though this rejection is real). Jesus focused on what gave positive meaning to his suffering. This is part of what empowered him to endure.

As you think about sanctification as a whole—both purification and endurance—remember one more thing: sanctification is a process. Give yourself the freedom to grow rather than expecting yourself to have arrived because you've understood some things. This is another way to protect your heart in the process of growing so that you experience sanctification as the gift God intends it to be.

QUESTIONS FOR REFLECTION

1. When and how have you experienced sanctification via purification as the only aspect of what it means to become more like Jesus?

2. How does understanding sanctification via endurance create more emotional freedom and motivation to grow in Christlikeness in response to hardships?

Chapter 25

GLORIFICATION
FINALLY, A PLACE OF REST

The final major theme of the gospel is glorification. This is when theologians talk about heaven, which can seem a bit far off. But glorification also has significance for the here and now. To understand the here-and-now implications of glorification, we may need to expand how we think about heaven.

THREE CONCEPTIONS OF HEAVEN

The Bible emphasizes many different things about heaven. At different points in our lives, each aspect of heaven brings a unique comfort. We will consider three aspects of heaven: splendor, purity, and rest. The third aspect will be our primary focus as a source of hope for our journey through grief.

First, heaven is a place of splendor. The splendor of heaven is a contrast to the finitude and scarcity of earth. Here we worry about shortages of money, food, and shelter. Heaven is a place with streets of gold, wedding feasts, and mansions. In heaven, we will lack nothing and will have no reason for worry.

Second, heaven is a place of purity. The purity of heaven is a contrast to the effects of sin within and around us on earth. Here we are aware of our own moral deficiencies and brace ourselves against the moral deficiencies of others. We live knowing the devil is like a crouching lion waiting to devour us and those we love (1 Peter 5:8). In heaven, we will be completely free from the fear that arises from the presence of sin. In heaven, we will remember the fear of sin the way adults remember their childhood fear of monsters under their bed.

Third, heaven is a place of rest. The rest that heaven offers is a contrast to the wearying effects of suffering we experience now. While we frequently allude to the reality that Jesus will wipe away every tear upon our arrival in heaven (Revelation 21:4), I am not sure we squeeze all the juice from this truth. This promise is more than a won't-that-be-nice image of what is in store for us in heaven.

The fact that heaven is a place of rest means that rest—settledness, peacefulness, and all that is meant by the Hebrew word *shalom*—is what God desires for us. In the same way that God wants purity for us on earth, God also wants peace for us. We are not being selfish to long for this rest any more than we are being vain to long for a conscience free from guilt. Our longing for peace echoes God's heart for us. The time we devote to seeking peace is an investment God affirms. Because our journey has been primarily about processing suffering, we will consider the eternal and temporal significance of the rest aspect of glorification.

THE ETERNAL SIGNIFICANCE OF GLORIFICATION

When we read that Jesus wipes away every tear, we notice that those being welcomed into heaven have been crying. Jesus's instinct is to come near them. He notices their pain. He is tender in his approach. Much of what causes our unrest after suffering is how seldom we get these responses from those around us. Too often when we are hurting, people pull away, look away, and show their discomfort. This adds to our hurt. Heaven will be nothing like this.

If your unrest is exacerbated by the nagging question, Will I ever be understood? the answer is yes! In fact, God even understands our pain that is too deep for words (Romans 8:26). The Holy Spirit is translating the cries we can't articulate to the Father. This is nice, but often we do not have a felt sense of this being true. In heaven, we will live with a perpetual sense of being fully understood, fully known, and fully loved. The unrest of feeling stigmatized and misunderstood will evaporate (see the Additional Resources appendix on page 158 for more on this topic).

The work we have done together has been part of answering the phrase in the Lord's prayer where we ask that things be "on earth as [they are] in heaven" (Matthew 6:10). As with any answer to this prayer, our current experience is partial. But we pray with confidence knowing that what we are asking is God's will. Any incremental growth toward this reality is something to be celebrated. I pray our journey together has advanced how much you feel understood on earth as you will be heaven.

THE TEMPORAL SIGNIFICANCE OF GLORIFICATION

But we must also ask, How does glorification impact the remaining, pre-heaven part of our experience? I will use another comparison. Imagine a season of your life when you had more to do than time to get it all done. Remember how you felt when you laid down at night. You were exhausted. You wanted sleep. You didn't feel like you had time to sleep, so you felt guilty. You felt conflicted about embracing the very thing you needed. This tension detracted from the replenishing effect God wanted sleep to have.

This is an image of how many of us respond to embracing the recuperation process after painful experiences. We can tell we're hurt. We want to heal. But we feel selfish for investing in the work healing requires. But as the pain causes anger and despair to leak into other areas of life, we realize we have no choice.

That may capture how you felt at the beginning of this journey. If so, you probably found it difficult to gain traction in the early part of this book. Understanding the rest aspect of glorification helps us set these concerns aside and embrace what God desires for us.

Go back to the sleep analogy. Imagine it is not you who are excessively busy and tired but a friend. Imagine you come over to help them, and as you walk in to see what they want you to do next, you find them asleep midtask. How do you feel about their rest? You are grateful they are getting what they need. You smile with fondness that their tenacity gave way to their humanity. You pray that this rest is as restorative as possible. You hope they wake up feeling refreshed rather than guilty for having slept.

That scene illustrates my intent for our journey together: that you recognize that God is this kind of friend (Exodus 33:11). My hope is that you have realized that the anger you felt in your grief was something you could share with God, and I pray that walking the journey with him has brought relief, comfort, and rest for your soul.

QUESTIONS FOR REFLECTION

1. Which of the three conceptions of heaven is most beneficial for processing the painful things you have experienced?

2. What metaphor would you use to describe how you relate to the rest that God wants to offer you as a means of recovery from the painful things you have experienced?

Appendix

ADDITIONAL RESOURCES FROM AUTHOR BRAD HAMBRICK AND OTHERS

FINDING A COUNSELOR

"How to Find a Good Counselor in [Name of City], July 15, 2016, http://bradhambrick.com/findacounselor/.

GUIDANCE ON GOOD MENTAL HEALTH

"50 Good Mental Health Habits," May 8, 2018, http://bradhambrick.com/50mhh/.

PARENTING TEENAGERS

Using psalms such as Psalm 44, "'Papa's an Idiot' Letter and Heretical Psalms," August 2, 2016, http://bradhambrick.com/papas-an-idiot-letter-and-heretical-psalms/.

PROCESSING SUFFERING

"Making Peace with Romans 8:28," July 25, 2019, http://bradhambrick.com/romans828/.

THE RELATIONSHIP BETWEEN TRUST AND FORGIVENESS

"When Talking about Forgiveness: A Guide for Christian Conversations and Ministry," February 13, 2020, http://bradhambrick.com/forgiveness/, particularly articles 12–14 in this series, which are excerpts from his book *Making Sense of Forgiveness* (Greensboro, NC: New Growth Press, 2021).

"Is Embracing Forgiveness from Others Harder Than from God?" May 14, 2020, http://bradhambrick.com/forgiveness18.

TRAUMA AND THE POST-TRAUMATIC EXPERIENCE

"Post-Traumatic Stress," seminar videos, September 25 2015, www.bradhambrick.com/ptsd.

WRESTLING WITH CYNICISM

Dick Keyes, *Seeing Through Cynicism: A Reconsideration of the Power of Suspicion* (Downers Grove, IL: IVP, 2006).

bradhambrick.com

ENDNOTES

1. J. R. R. Tolkien, *The Hobbit: 75th Anniversary Edition* (Boston: Houghton Mifflin Harcourt, 2012), 107.

2. C. S. Lewis, *The Magician's Nephew* (New York: Scholastic, 1988), 142.